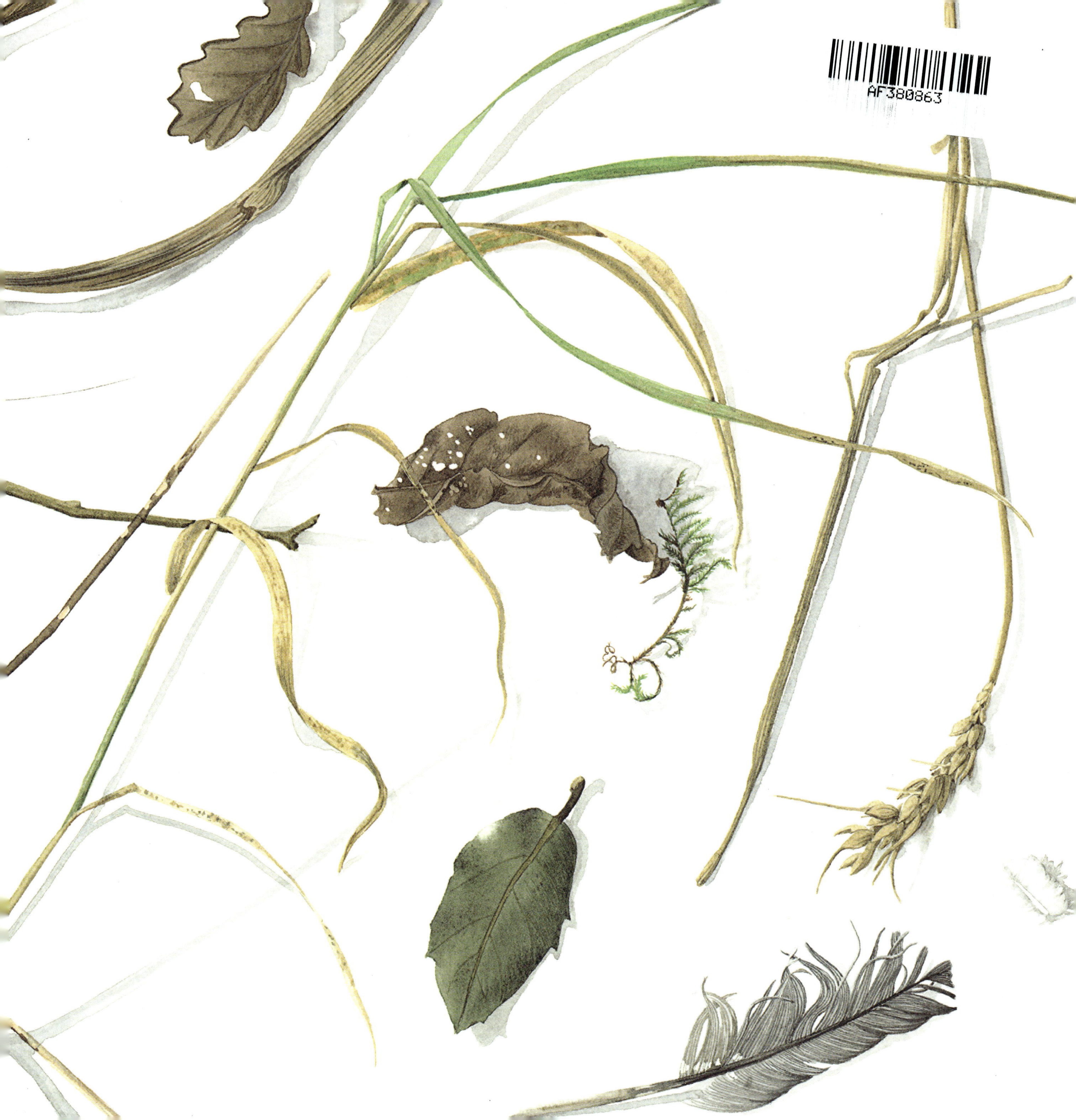

AF380863

NESTS

NESTS

SUSAN OGILVY

PARTICULAR BOOKS

NOTE

In the making of this collection, great care has been taken
not to disturb nesting birds. All the nests were either old and
abandoned, or else new but displaced by strong winds or
predators. It was once considered perfectly acceptable
to gather birds' eggs – indeed many amateur naturalists had
such collections. But it became apparent that some bird
populations were in decline, partly as a result of this hobby,
and in 1981 the Wildlife and Countryside Act made it
a crime to collect wild birds' eggs and to disturb nesting birds.
It is nowadays unthinkable for any bird lover to violate
the nests of these remarkable creatures.

All the nests in this book are shown at life size.

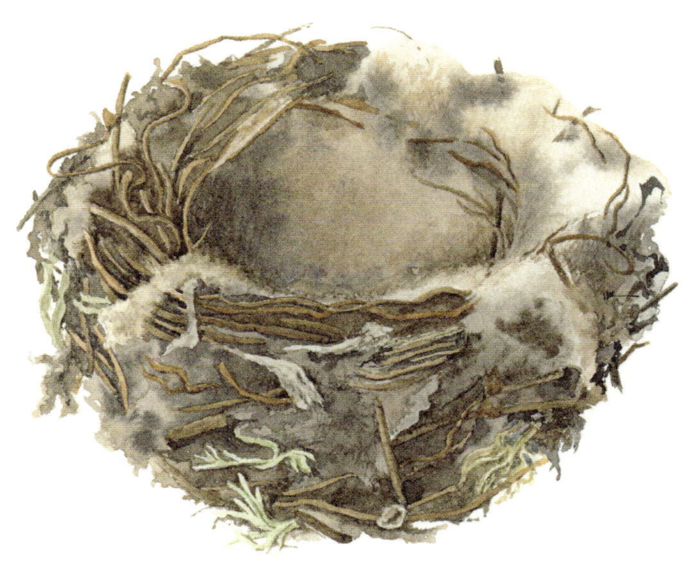

Goldcrest *Regulus regulus*

One day, while clearing up the garden after a storm,
I found a chaffinch nest – it was a strange, sodden
lump lying on the grass under a fir tree, and I wasn't
even sure what it was. I brought it inside, placed it on a
newspaper and over the next few hours, as the weight of water
drained out of it, the sodden lump blossomed into a jewel-like
nest, reminding me of the wonder of those tiny Japanese paper
flowers that emerged from shells placed in water, which had
enchanted me as a child. The nest was clearly very new and
unfinished, as the lining of feathers was sparse and the moss
was fresh. I was enthralled, and dropped everything to paint it.

This was the start of a fascination with nests. Until
I found this perfect object, I'd not realized how diverse nest
building is, nor the skill with which they are built. Each species
has its own method, favouring certain materials – twigs, roots,
grasses, leaves, moss, lichen, hair, feathers and cobwebs – that
reflect its habitat. The reed bunting, for instance, lines its nest
with the fluff of pulled-apart reed mace, while the blue tit nest
that I found on the Isle of Arran includes deer hair – an abundant
material on the island. Some birds incorporate what we humans
might call rubbish, and the best example I know is that of
a friend whose father came in from the garden, when she was
a child, carrying a nest that contained one of her name tapes.

As a botanical illustrator I have made a point of only
ever painting from life, never from photographs, or even my
own notes. So the collection here is entirely due to chance,
initially depending upon any abandoned nests I came across

in the garden or on walks. But gradually, as I progressed,
word got out that I was painting nests, and family and friends
brought me finds of their own. I was able to learn a good deal
through my own observations, but as my fascination with nests
grew, I wanted to learn much more about them. I came up
against a surprising lack of books about nest building, however,
and could find no modern works specifically on the subject
of British and European birds' nests. My father was a lifelong
lover of birds, and among his old books I found Charles
A. Hall's *Birds' Eggs and Nests*, published in 1932, which he had
received as a birthday present when he was fourteen, and this
seemed to be the last word. My eldest son later gave me *British
Birds' Nests* by Richard Kearton, dating from 1895. By this time
I had painted about ten nests, and it was dawning on me that
eyes need to be opened to these wonderful works of avian
architecture – perhaps I might even produce a book of my own?

At about this stage in the project a friend introduced
me to Deon Warner. Deon has for many years carried out the
British Trust for Ornithology surveys in the part of Somerset
where we both live, and spends hours of every day walking
and watching. He embraced my project with great enthusiasm
and kindness and over the next few years brought me many
nests – usually ones he had spotted and watched through the
summers and collected once the nesting season was over and
the nests had been abandoned. He has a vast knowledge on all
wildlife, and I could not have 'sat at the feet' of anyone better.
Deon's tall, rangy, white-haired figure must be known for miles

around as he walks the county, sometimes pausing to listen to birdsong. Once I had painted a batch of nests I'd take them back to Deon, show him the paintings and then sit in his sitting room – which looks like a branch of the Natural History Museum – and learn. When the Covid pandemic arrived and such visits were forbidden, we would stand outside one or other house and continue the conversation. This book would have been almost impossible without him, and I am for ever grateful for his friendship and his teaching.

My exploration of nests has been limited by serendipity, but it has also been limited by scale, as I prefer to obey the rules of botanical illustration and paint to life-size. As the idea of a book took hold, it became a necessity that the nests should fit on the page of a reasonably sized volume. (Actually, a couple of nests extend beyond the edge of the page, but the bowl of those nests is within the margins.) This restriction has meant that I've concentrated on the passerines, the common garden birds throughout Britain and much of Europe, Scandinavia and as far afield as Russia, Turkey and North Africa. Some of these are resident; others are migrants who come to Britain to breed but spend their winters in warmer climes.

The Passeriformes are the largest order of birds, with more than five thousand species, represented on all continents except Antarctica. They are perching birds, having feet with three forward-facing toes and one backward-facing, which enables them to grasp twigs and branches. Within this order are the Oscines – the songbirds. Passerines are generally more active by day, roosting at night. Their chicks hatch at an early stage in their development, when they are frail, naked and need much parental care. This informs the parent birds' nest design,

as protection from both the weather and predators is required. Non-passerines such as ducks, geese and swans make their nests on the ground as their young hatch at a more advanced stage of development and are more able to fend for themselves.

Nests can largely be divided into four types: the cup, the dome, the scrape and the burrow or cavity. Most passerines use the architecture of the cup or dome – exceptions include nightjars and skylarks, which nest in shallow depressions on the ground such as the prints left by cows' hoofs, or in tufts of grass, and woodpeckers, which nest in holes in tree trunks. The shape of each species' nest is determined by its habitat and the needs of its young. An abundance of predators will mean that good camouflage is required; strong prevailing winds will perhaps dictate the need for a domed nest; the instinctive urge for a bird to build in caves may be satisfied by building within barns or the eaves of roofs.

Cup-shaped nests vary in depth, but are perfectly suited to the needs of both the eggs and the nestlings. The eggs are held together in a cluster by the bowl of the cup so that the incubating adult can cover them all efficiently. When the eggs hatch, the naked, blind nestlings are held together for mutual warmth, and the depth of the cup means they are less likely to fall from the nest (although when this does happen the adult birds will usually continue to care for the chick on the ground). Domed nests provide even better shelter for the nestlings. The long-tailed tit's pear-shaped nest is much admired for this facility. Made largely of moss and cobwebs, with a side entrance hole near the top, the tensile strength of the cobwebs means that the 'bag' is elastic and can expand as the chicks grow.

The position and bulk of each nest are also influenced by climate. Birds living in the cold north or at high elevations have generally heavier nests, with thicker walls and better insulation than those that live in warmer climes or at lower altitudes. These warmer nests are also more common among birds who breed early in the nesting season. A woodpecker will orientate its nest so that the entrance hole faces the sun, while birds with domed nests will make the side entrance face away from the wind. Height from the ground may be determined by the threat of predators and the available camouflage. Hawthorn hedges and bramble thickets are favoured nesting sites for many small birds, as the thorns deter predators.

In order to understand its structure, a nest can be divided into layers – although not all birds use all layers. The main layer is the strongest, providing the framework for the others. On the outside camouflage or decoration may be added, while the inside is generally lined with a soft, insulating layer for the protection of the chicks. The other component is the attachment to the branch or twigs on which the bird has chosen to build. This is generally incorporated into the main structural layer so, while fundamental, it is not obvious to the observer. It may take the form of the twigs and roots used in the structural layer of the nests of birds like blackbirds and thrushes, while other birds, such as finches, rely on the strength of cobwebs to attach their nests. Goldfinch nests are built towards the end of branches, where they sway with the wind, but although they look very precarious they are firmly anchored.

The materials with which birds make their nests are determined by instinct, availability and location. The possibilities are endless, and it is here that the real ingenuity of each species can be most clearly observed by the layman. The architecture will remain distinctively that of the species to which the nest belongs, but serendipity comes into play here, too, and birds show a remarkable ability to adapt, make do and invent.

As I painted, I found myself wondering how a bird starts to build a nest. I've never found the answer – and on the whole I am happy with that. Piles of loose twigs have often been noticed under rookeries – evidence of false starts. But how, for instance, a tiny reed warbler persuades two heavy reed stems together with her first piece of grass remains a mystery to me. Leaving this puzzle to one side, however, we can move on to the materials. Here, the range is vast. Birds building in cities will use all sorts of bits and pieces that their rural cousins wouldn't need. Among the goldfinch nests in this book is one found in London that contains a lot of upholstery materials, which make an excellent substitute for the fine rootlets, wool and thistledown used in the goldfinch nests found in Somerset. By the same token, I've found a surprising amount of baler twine in rural nests, usually unravelled into fine strands.

Most people think of nests as twiggy structures, but birds also commonly use grasses and moss, preferring young, new twigs and grasses that are pliable and easier to manipulate. The same goes for the fine roots favoured by some birds, such as bullfinches. Blackbirds and thrushes add mud and strips of bark to their structures. The wide use of spiders' webs surprised me at first. But they have adhesive qualities and, as is well known, the tensile strength of spider silk is comparable to that of high grade steel, so it is a perfect material with which to build a secure, lightweight nest – and how brilliant of birds to know that!

The decorative, or camouflage, layer is added once the structure is complete and, again, is dictated by location. Many birds use moss and lichen for this purpose while robins, for example, prefer dried leaves. Wrens' nests are wonderful creations, ingeniously built into well-hidden spaces, and all seem to include moss. Some birds do not form an outer layer at all.

The nest's lining is, of course, as crucial as its structure, as this is what will protect the nestlings from cold and harm. Of all British birds that line their nests only the song thrush does not use soft materials. Instead it makes a paste of rotten wood and saliva, which is then moulded into a lining by the hen bird, as she circles round and round within the cup, smoothing the paste against the twiggy outer structure with her breast. The end result resembles papier-mâché. Other birds use a variety of fine grasses, sheep wool, hair and plant fibres, depending upon their habitat. Finches, which are seed eaters, use the fibres of unopened dandelion clocks to line their nests, while reed buntings, who nest near water, will use pulled apart bulrushes.

Some birds, such as pigeons and doves, leave their nests unlined. Collared dove nests are rather shambolic, twiggy structures that are built high in a tree, and because they are not lined the eggs can be seen through the twigs from the ground. By contrast the long-tailed tit lines its nest with hundreds of tiny, downy feathers. Some birds will use feathers from any species, while others use only their own. During the breeding season many birds shed, or sometimes pluck, the soft downy feathers at the middle of their bellies in order to produce a bare patch of skin known as the 'brood patch'. The parent bird settles itself in such a way as to rest the bare skin directly on the surface of the eggs, thus transferring body heat more efficiently. The feathers from this area of the parent bird's body make ideal nest lining and regrow once the season is over.

Once the nest is finished the hen lays her eggs, one a day, but only starts incubating them when her clutch is complete, which means that they'll all hatch at roughly the same time and will be fed and nurtured as a complete family. Some birds, such as herons, owls and birds of prey, lay their eggs on alternate days but start incubation with the first egg, so their clutch contains nestlings at varying stages of development. The number of eggs and the length of the incubation period vary between species. The hatchlings eat a vast amount and grow very fast, keeping the parents extremely busy gathering provisions, which is why most birds nest within reach of their favoured food sources. Within two or three weeks most have fledged – that is, they have left the nest, although they generally stay within its vicinity and continue to be fed by the parents for a few days or weeks more.

Over the next months the fledglings develop into fully independent juveniles, then sub-adults, and finally into adults, with full plumage and the ability to reproduce. Many species produce more than one clutch per season, sometimes re-using the original nest after a bit of refurbishment. Others will build a whole new nest, sometimes within the first one.

By September the breeding and nesting season in Britain is over for another year. Migratory birds feed well in the autumn in order to build up their body reserves before departing. The swallow is perhaps the best known migrant, and the sight of great flocks of them gathering on telegraph wires is common in Britain in September. They travel up to two hundred miles a day, down through France and Spain, over into Morocco, across the Sahara and into South Africa and Namibia on a journey that takes about six weeks. Millions of birds perform this extraordinary feat year after year – many of them warblers, such as chiffchaffs, whitethroats and reed warblers. Meanwhile our resident birds congregate in large flocks and, finding safety in numbers, roam the countryside feeding on seeds, grain, berries and insects. They need large amounts of food to sustain themselves through the long cold nights, which they often spend huddled together in roosts of many dozens of birds, sometimes crowded into old nests or crevices. I have noticed that the old house martin nests in the porch of our village church have been appropriated in cold weather. Eventually winter passes, the migrants return, and so another nesting season comes around.

Sometimes I've been asked how I go about the task of painting a nest. It is not an easy question to answer. The most important part of botanical painting is looking, and as I look I plan where to start. I paint with watercolour on Hot Pressed paper, using fine, good quality sable brushes. I set the nest up on a couple of old, paper-covered bricks as close as possible to the front of my drawing board, with a piece of white card behind to act as a sight screen. Then I start by measuring the nest with calipers, making small pencil marks on the paper to ensure that the painting will be life-sized. I begin by drawing the 'landmark' pieces of the nest in fine, careful lines, before I paint them, and then continue this rhythm of drawing and painting, getting ever more deeply into the nest as I go. Sometimes, once I'm fully absorbed, I draw straight onto the paper with paint and don't bother to switch back and forth between pencil and paintbrush. I find I can only do about an hour and a half at a sitting before I need a break, so I'll go and do something else for half an hour before returning. For the very fine detail I use a large, old magnifying glass that once belonged to my husband's grandfather and has, over the years, become a much treasured piece of my equipment. Painting a nest takes several days and is as immersive as a jigsaw puzzle; and with the radio in the background providing commentary on an equally absorbing test match, it is about as perfect a way to spend the time as I can imagine.

It is widely acknowledged that a good painting is more useful to a botanist than a photograph. Given the sophistication of modern photography, this is hard to explain. It may be something to do with the careful observation which has informed the image – perhaps even the love which has been put into it – that results in a clearer representation than a photograph and so is of more use to a scientist. I hope the fact that these nest portraits have been painted by someone used to the demands of botanical illustration will mean that they are shown with a clarity that will do justice to their creators and open readers' eyes to their wonders.

I've said that this book started with the chaffinch nest I found in my garden – and in a sense it did – but I had been well aware of birds and nests long before that particular discovery. A large part of my childhood was spent abroad, because my father was in the army. He loved birds all his life and, wherever we lived, he rarely went for a walk without his binoculars hanging round his neck. In due course my brother followed in his footsteps, and family drives would be punctuated by the car screeching to a halt and my father and Crispin leaping out to plunge into a thicket, while my mother, sister and I rolled our eyes and looked at our watches. Perhaps we were so force-fed with birds that we simply left them to the menfolk, and this is why it has taken me so long to make an effort to learn about them. Although somewhat late in the day, it has been a huge pleasure and I have felt my father beside me through it all. I found the reed warbler nest, very old and dry, in his study when I cleared it after his death, and this book is dedicated to him, with my love.

TO THE MEMORY OF
DONALD EASTEN
1918–2017

COLLARED DOVE

Streptopelia decaocto

Resident	
Lifespan	Up to 10 years
Diet	Grain, seeds, berries
Breeding season	March to August
Broods	3–5 clutches of 2 eggs
Position	In trees or climbing plants at a height from 1.5 to 20 metres
Materials	Twigs
Lining	None

Collared dove nests are surprisingly flimsy, but this one is slightly more sparse than usual as it was found several months after it had been used and had lost some of its structure. The twigs used by the collared dove are long and unwieldy – one in this nest was 60cm long.

Essentially, the nest is not much more than a loose, twiggy platform. The hen lays two eggs and both parents share the incubation of about fourteen to eighteen days; since the nest is unlined, it's possible to see the eggs from below. The young are fed for the first ten days on crop milk – a secretion produced in the crops of both parent birds – before they fledge at about twelve to nineteen days. The parents go on caring for their fledglings for another week or so after they have left the nest and before they become fully independent. Collared doves have between three and five broods in a year.

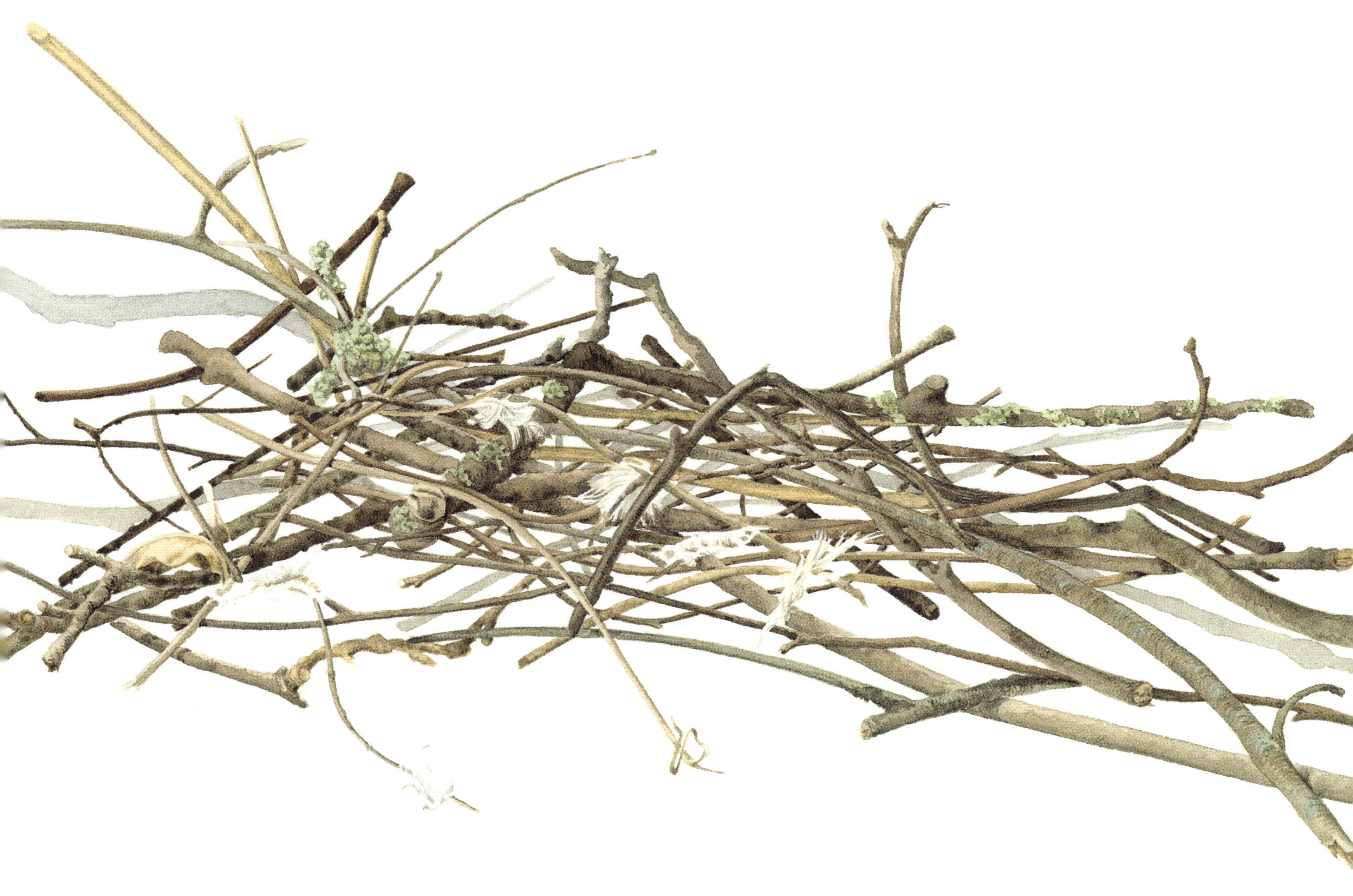

COLLARED DOVE

Streptopelia decaocto

This collared dove's nest is far more bulky than the one on the previous page, as it is three nests deep. The first nest would have been a relatively scanty platform, and for each subsequent clutch of eggs the dove has added another layer of twigs. In the process of housing all these families it has also accumulated a fair number of droppings, which have added to the bulk. Deon Warner found this specimen high up in a tree and watched it through the summer as three clutches were raised, with the nest refurbished for each family, so that the nest he collected in the winter was the substantial structure you see here.

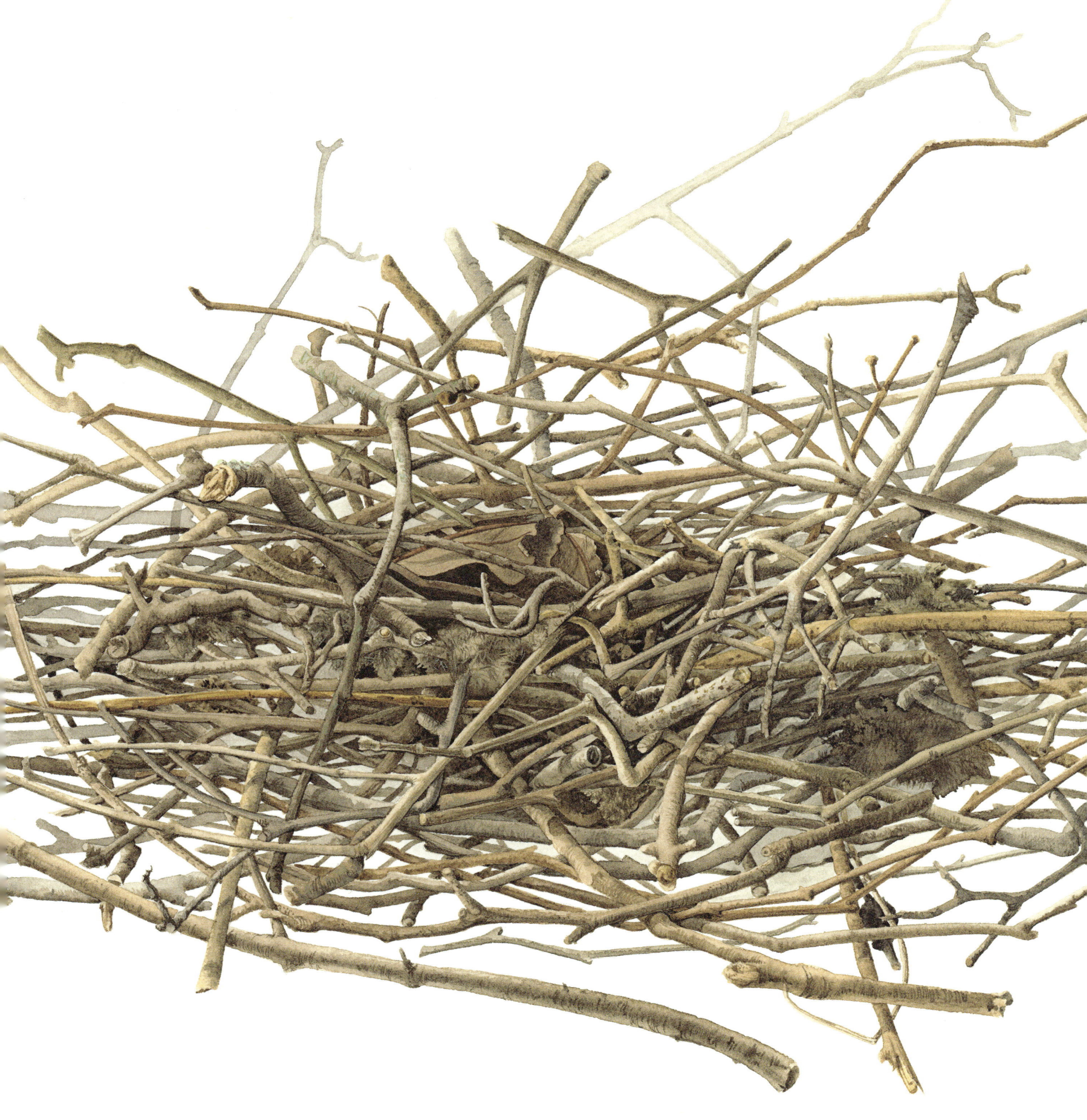

SWALLOW

Hirundo rustica

Migrant	Arrives in Britain from Africa in April; most have left by October
Lifespan	5–10 years, although more than 15 years has been recorded
Diet	Flying insects
Breeding season	May to August
Broods	2–3 clutches of 3–6 eggs
Position	Inside barns, porches, sheds
Materials	Mud, straw
Lining	Fine grass, feathers

The English saying of 'one swallow does not a summer make' tells us that this is a migrant from afar, arriving around mid-April from as far away as southern Africa. Swallows build their nests in barns, porches, under bridges or in other places that mimic their original cave habitat; in some places it is regarded as a sign of good fortune to have one attached to your house.

Both sexes make the nest of mud and straw stuck together with saliva, lining it with fine grasses and feathers. They frequently return from migration to re-use the previous year's nest. The female incubates the eggs for fourteen to sixteen days, and both parents feed the young for about three weeks. They will rear two or three broods in a season. In the autumn they fly south, feeding on the wing, and roosting in traditional sites at night.

My youngest son climbed up to remove this nest from inside the porch of our village hall. It had not been used for some years and was full of old leaves and grass, which Deon Warner later decided was likely to be the remains of a wren's nest built within the old swallow's nest.

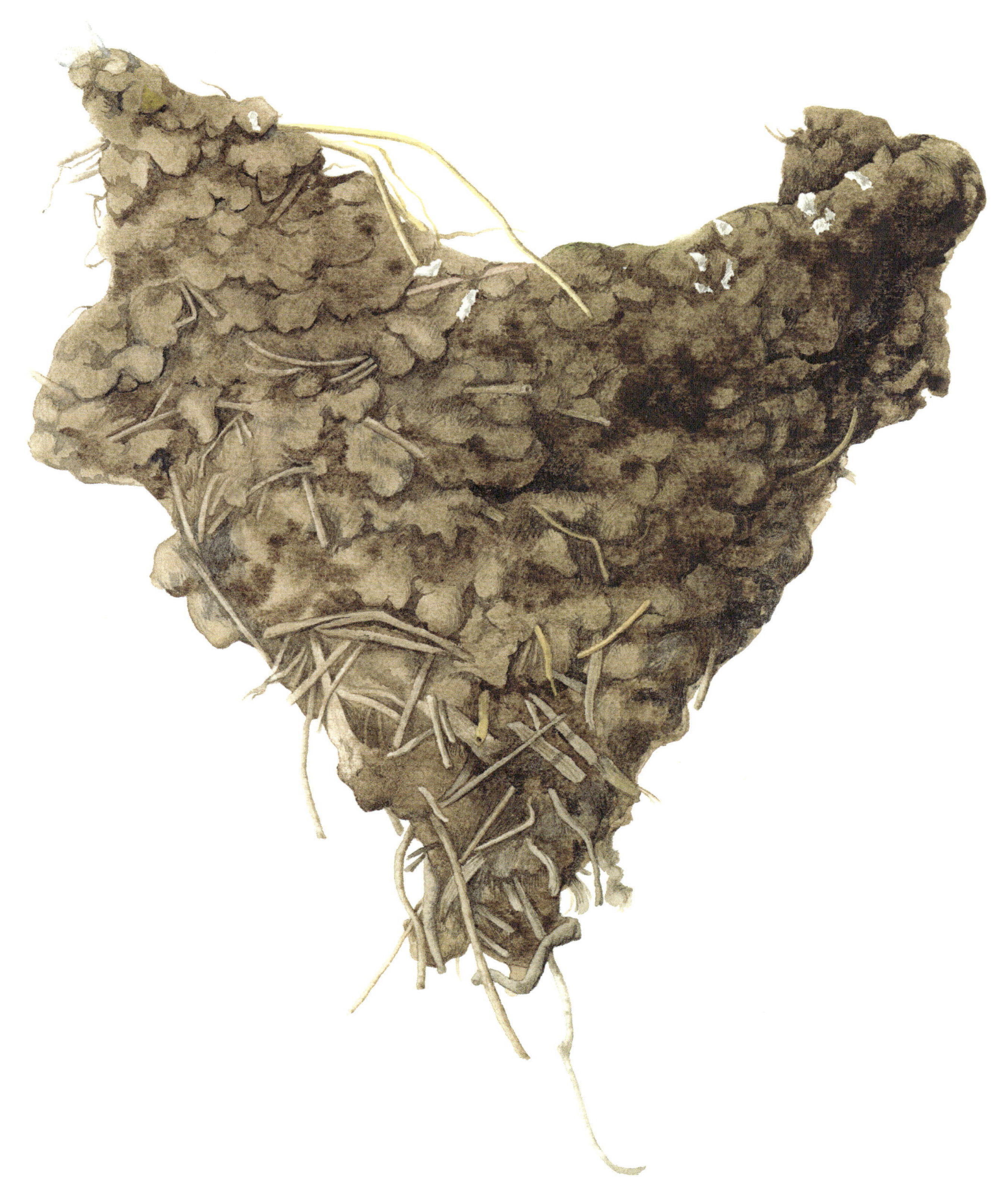

HOUSE MARTIN

Delichon urbica

Migrant	Arrives in Britain from Africa in late April or early May; leaves between August and October
Lifespan	5–10 years
Diet	Flying insects
Breeding season	May to August
Broods	2–3 clutches of 3–5 eggs
Position	Under the eaves of houses and barns, often in colonies
Materials	Mud, straw
Lining	Fine grass, feathers

Because the house martin spends the vast majority of its life in the air, there is something rather mysterious about it. We often see house martins perching on wires, but rarely on the ground. They feed on the wing on flying insects, and they may even sleep on the wing. Their legs and feet are very small, and they really only land in order to collect mud and grass for nest building. They often nest in colonies and re-use nests year after year.

Both adults build the nest, sharing the incubation of the eggs for about a fortnight and also the feeding of the nestlings. Most passerine fledglings are fed on the ground for around two weeks after leaving the nest, before they are ready to strike out on their own; but as the house martin is not naturally at home on the ground the fledglings return to the nest between their early flights and are fed there for another fortnight before finally leaving.

Because house martins frequently re-use their nests it is not usually possible to collect one. But this nest was so dilapidated that it had been taken over by house sparrows, who built a nest inside it. To paint it, I had to reconstruct the pieces of the shell of the nest, rather like mending a piece of china, but I hope it can be seen that the house martin nest is essentially a bowl made of mud pellets, built under the eaves of houses and barns and with a small entrance hole. The lining is a scant collection of grasses and sometimes feathers. It must be noted that the abundant feathers in this nest are those of the house sparrow's nest within it.

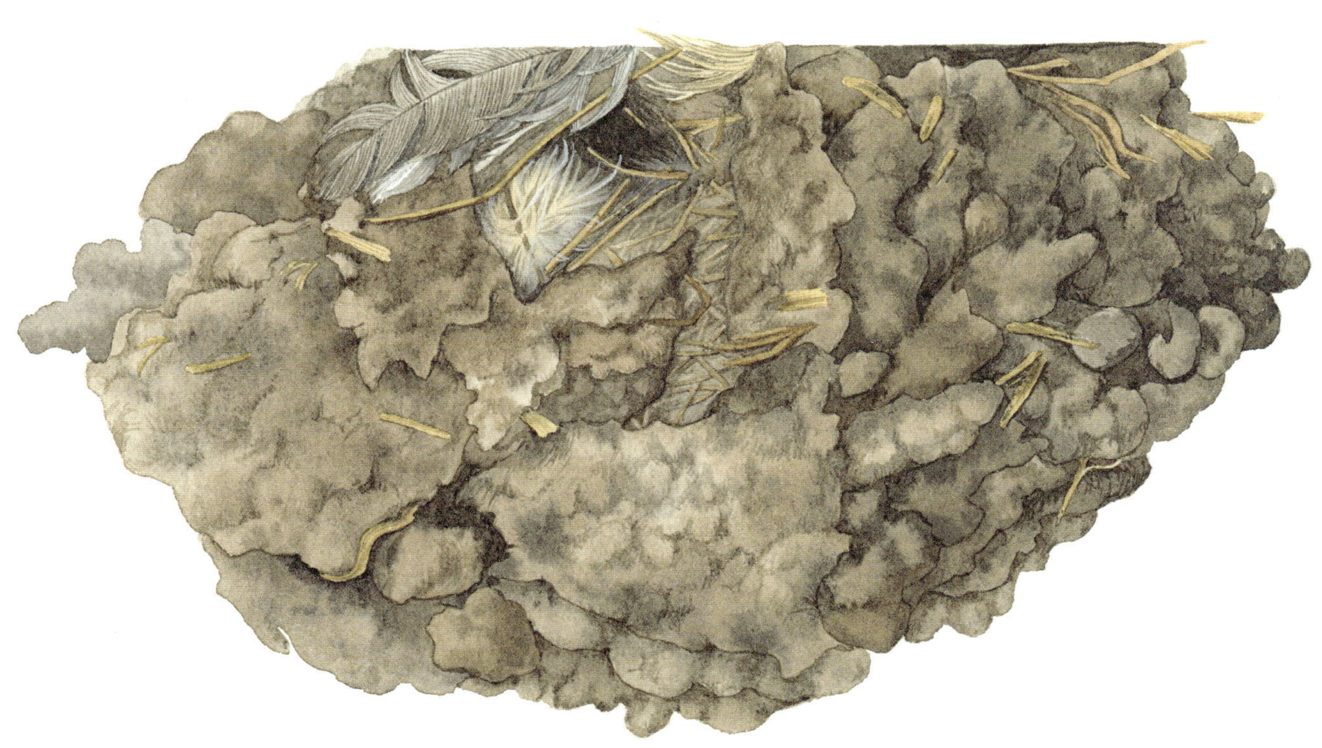

PIED WAGTAIL

Motacilla alba yarrellii

Resident	In harsh winters, northern pied wagtails may migrate to southern Britain
Lifespan	Up to 5 years
Diet	Insects
Breeding season	April to August
Broods	1–2 clutches of 3–8 eggs
Position	Usually in a crevice in a wall, bank or among stacks of logs or hay bales
Materials	Dry grass, leaves, fern fronds
Lining	Finer grasses, wool, horsehair, feathers, rabbit down

The pied wagtail, easily recognized by its constantly bobbing tail, enjoys a varied habitat and frequently favours sites near water. It often nests in holes and crevices in ditches and buildings, and sometimes adapts old nests from other species such as blackbirds – this nest was found among bales of hay.

Both sexes build the beautifully compact and intricate nest, with the female completing the lining of it with fine grasses, hair and feathers. The adults share the incubation of the eggs for about twelve days, then the feeding of the nestlings for another fortnight. The young continue to be fed for up to a week after they have fledged. In southern Britain pied wagtails often have two broods, although northern birds have only one.

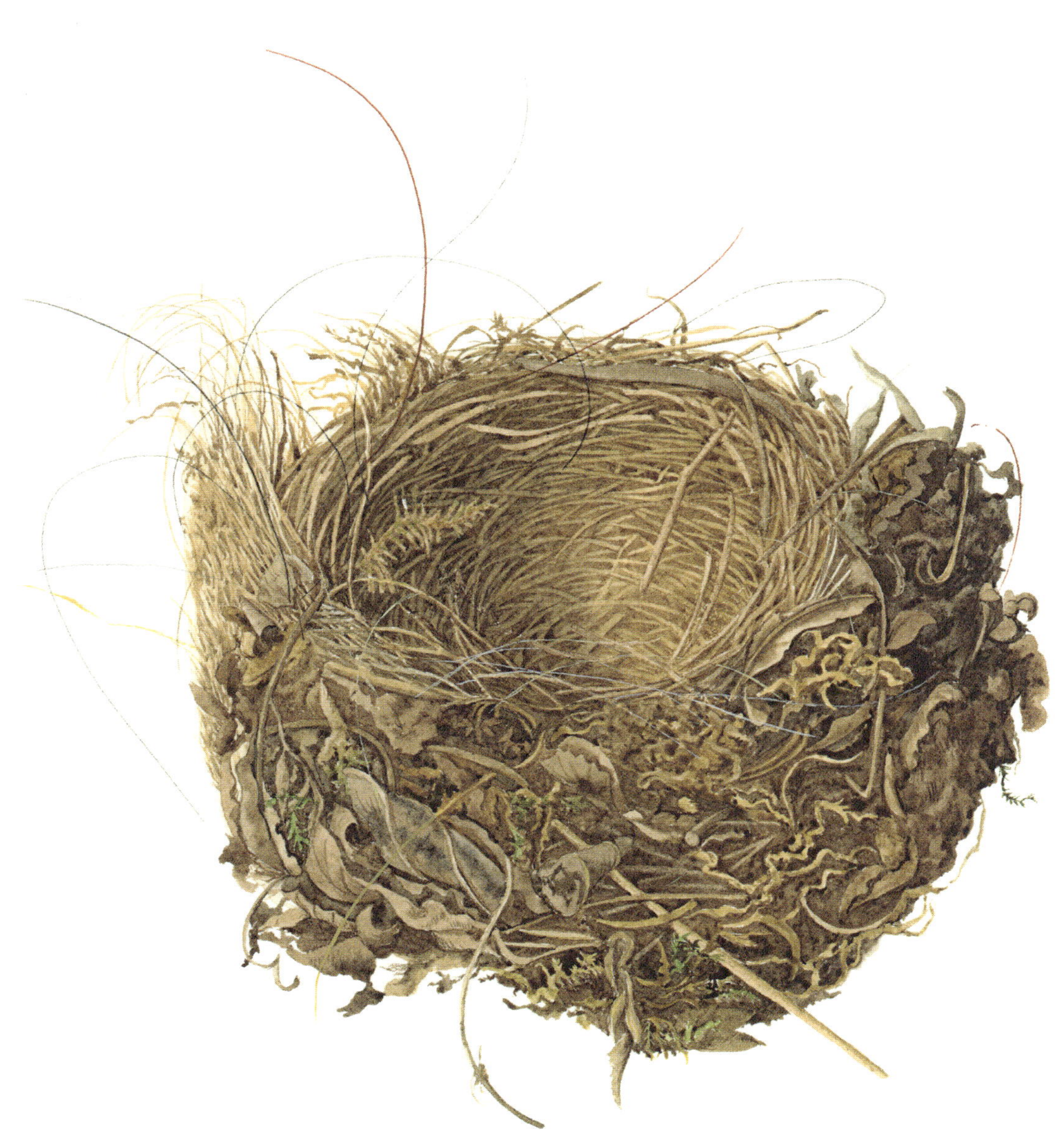

WREN

Troglodytes troglodytes

Resident

Lifespan — 3–5 years, although 6 years has been recorded

Diet — Insects

Breeding season — Late April to July

Broods — 1–2 clutches of 5–8 eggs

Position — In crevices, ivy-covered walls, etc.

Materials — Fine twigs, grasses, moss, skeleton leaves, feathers

Lining — Feathers, hair

The wren is a much loved little bird, admired for its loud and cheerful song which belies its diminutive size. It is also much admired for its nests.

These nests are built by the male. He builds between five and eight 'cock nests', all structurally complete but unlined, making use of the vegetation around his chosen site in order to camouflage it. How such a tiny bird can build so many large, domed nests and also go a-wooing is a marvel. Once his chosen mate has selected the nest she favours, she lines it with feathers and hair. She lays five to eight eggs (although up to sixteen have been recorded) and incubates them for fourteen to seventeen days. The male joins the feeding of the nestlings – although some males are polygamous and may have another brood to feed at the same time, in which case he will leave the hen to care for the first brood on her own.

The young fledge at between fourteen and nineteen days, and are usually cared for by both parents for a further week or two. They often have two broods. In the winter the wren copes with the cold nights by roosting with other wrens. As many as ninety-six have been recorded huddling together in one roost.

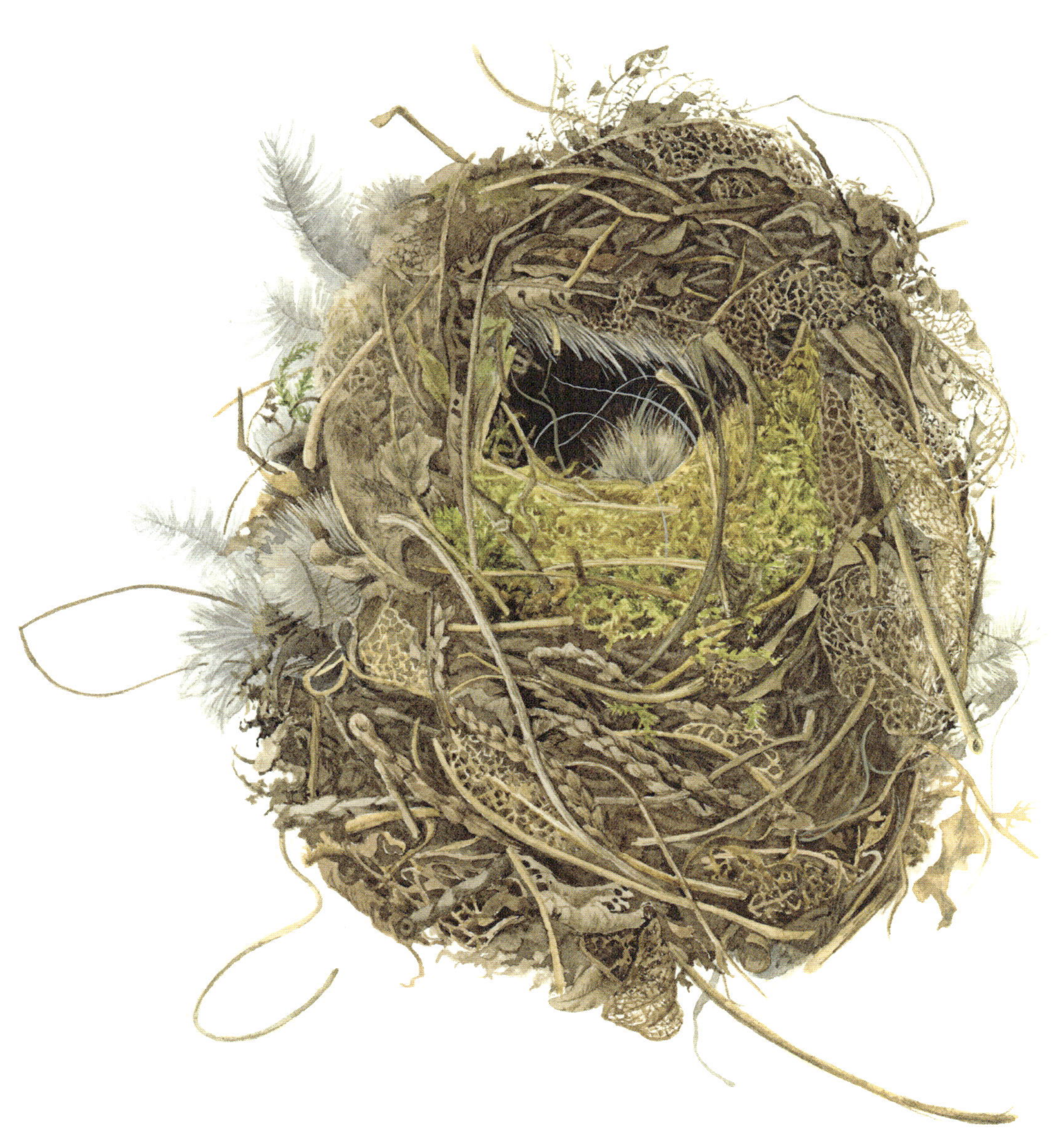

WREN

Troglodytes troglodytes

This nest was found in thick ivy on a wall. The architecture
is similar to the nest on the previous page, as is the use of moss
near the entrance, but here the wren has made use of the
ivy in which he has chosen to build by constructing his nest
within its branches.

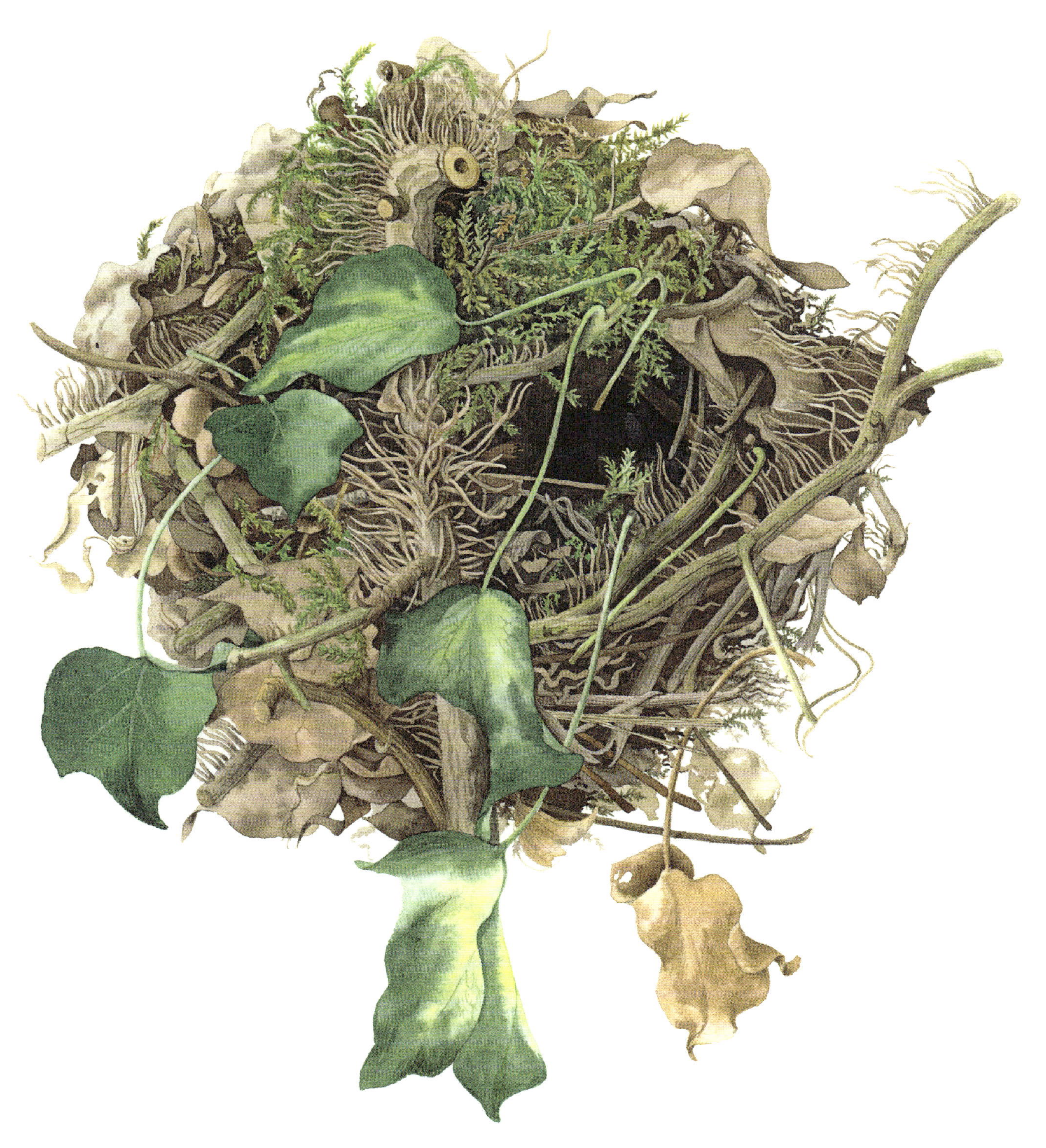

WREN

Troglodytes troglodytes

This wren's nest was built between two bales of straw that my eldest son had stored on an old bed base resting on the rafters of a barn. Once the nesting season was over I sat in the barn to paint it, and when I'd finished he parted the bales and removed the nest. It was surprisingly insubstantial, as the wren had made use of the space between the straw bales for the framework and simply lined and roofed it with moss and feathers.

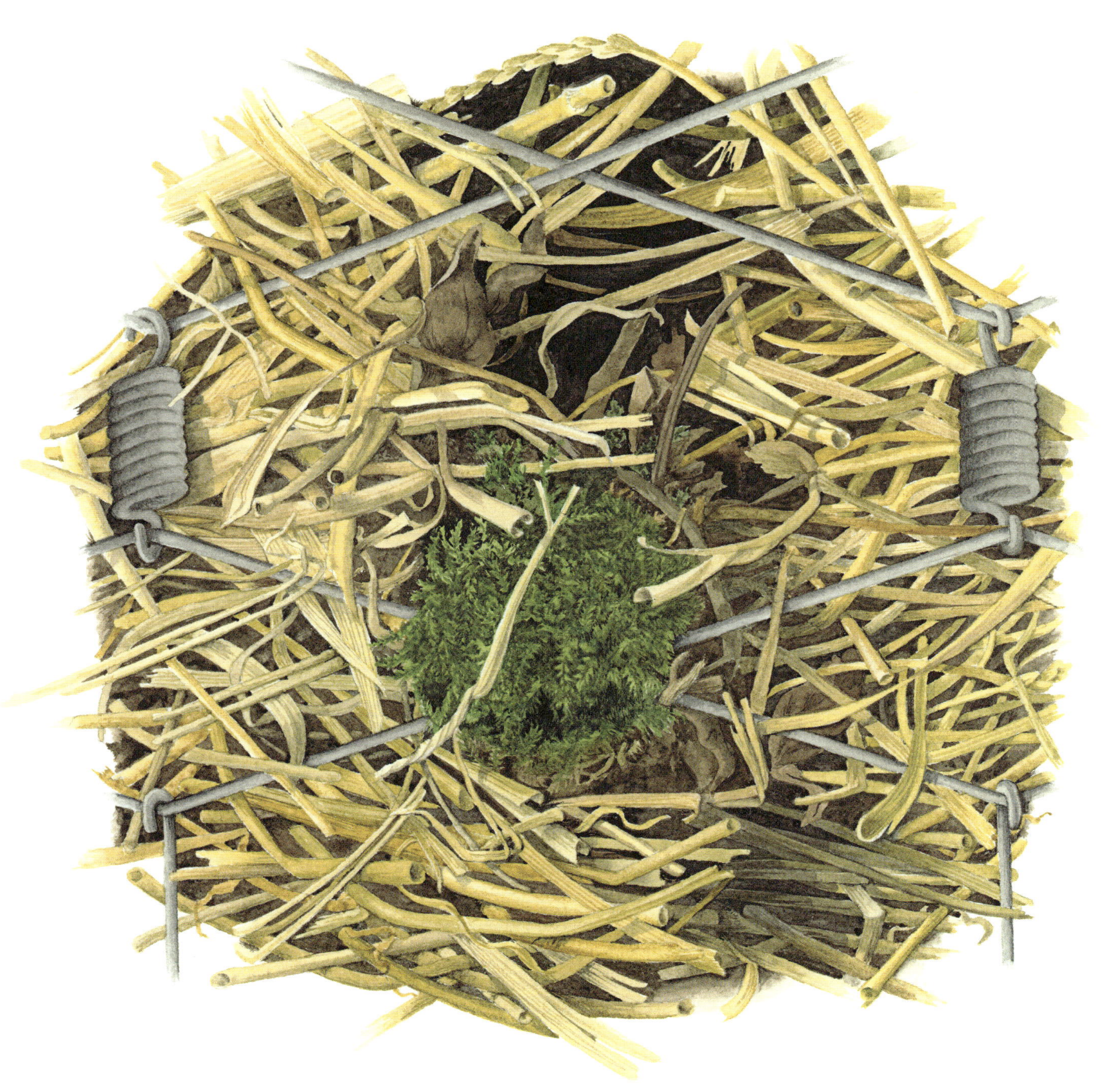

WREN

Troglodytes troglodytes

This cock nest is quite unlike any other wren's nest I have
seen, but it still demonstrates the species' instinctive domed
architecture. It was built over a couple of days in the corner
of a dog kennel, and used all the moss growing on the paved
path outside. Presumably the wren's lady love had misgivings
about the wisdom of living in a kennel, because the nest was
not lined or used.

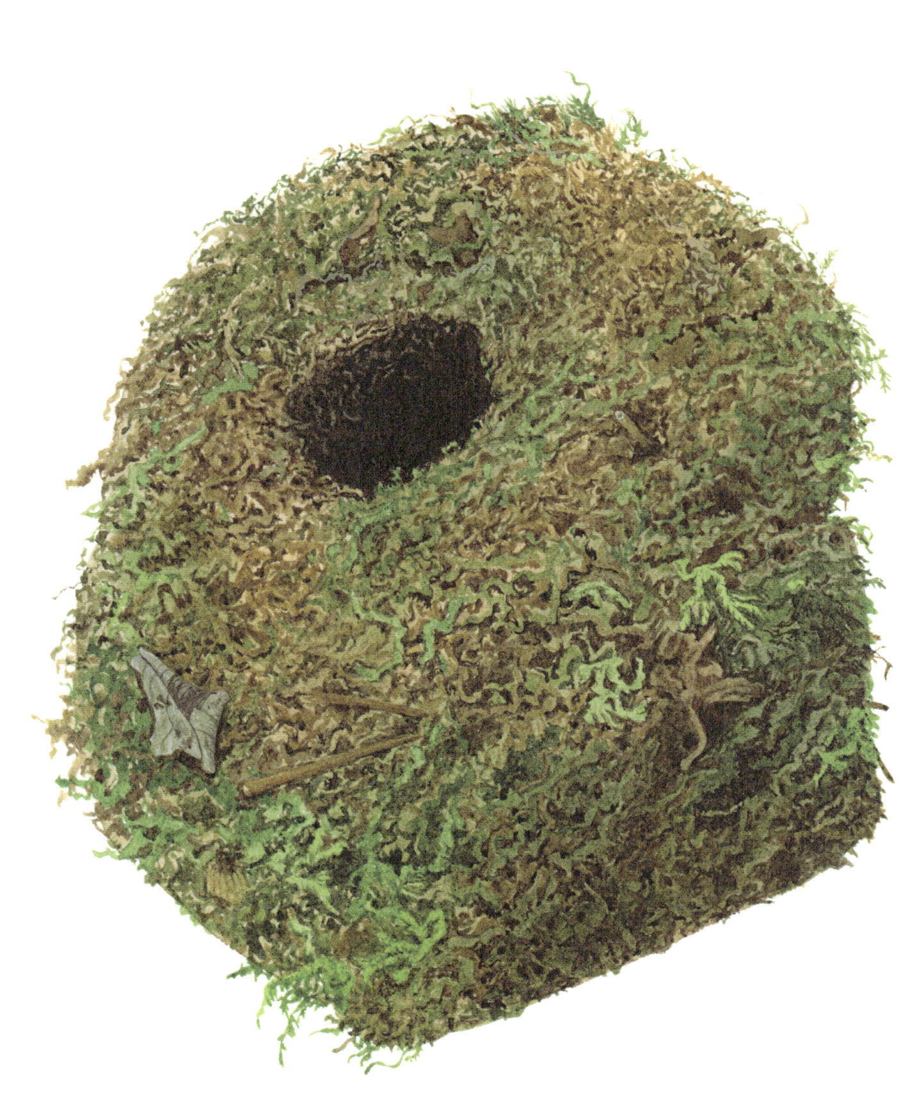

DUNNOCK
Prunella modularis

Resident	
Lifespan	About 5 years
Diet	Insects, seeds, berries, grain
Breeding season	April to July
Broods	1–3 clutches of 4–6 eggs
Position	Low down in bushes, hedges and bramble patches
Materials	Grass, moss, twigs, roots
Lining	Wool, moss, hair, sometimes feathers

Previously known as the hedge sparrow, the dunnock was renamed when it was found to belong to the Accentor family. The name comes from medieval English and means small brown bird – a perfect description for this modest, shy little creature. It is a widespread but sedentary species, seldom moving more than half a mile from its home territory. It nests near the ground, often in hawthorn hedges or brambles. But the timid dunnock has a complex mating system, with multiple partners, which can mean that the hen bird has more than one male to help feed her brood, thus increasing their chance of survival.

The female dunnock builds her nest between March and July, forming a deep cup of small twigs, grass, moss and rootlets, then lining it with feathers, wool, hair or moss. Sometimes she'll adapt an old nest from another bird. Dunnocks produce up to three broods per season, laying four to six eggs each time which the female incubates for twelve to thirteen days. The young leave the nest at twelve days. The dunnock nest is much favoured by the cuckoo.

This was the second nest I painted for this project. I was staying with my father at the time; his neighbour had found it in a hedge, and I painted it at the kitchen table. My father was then in his nineties and as fascinated by birds as ever, so he enjoyed the whole process.

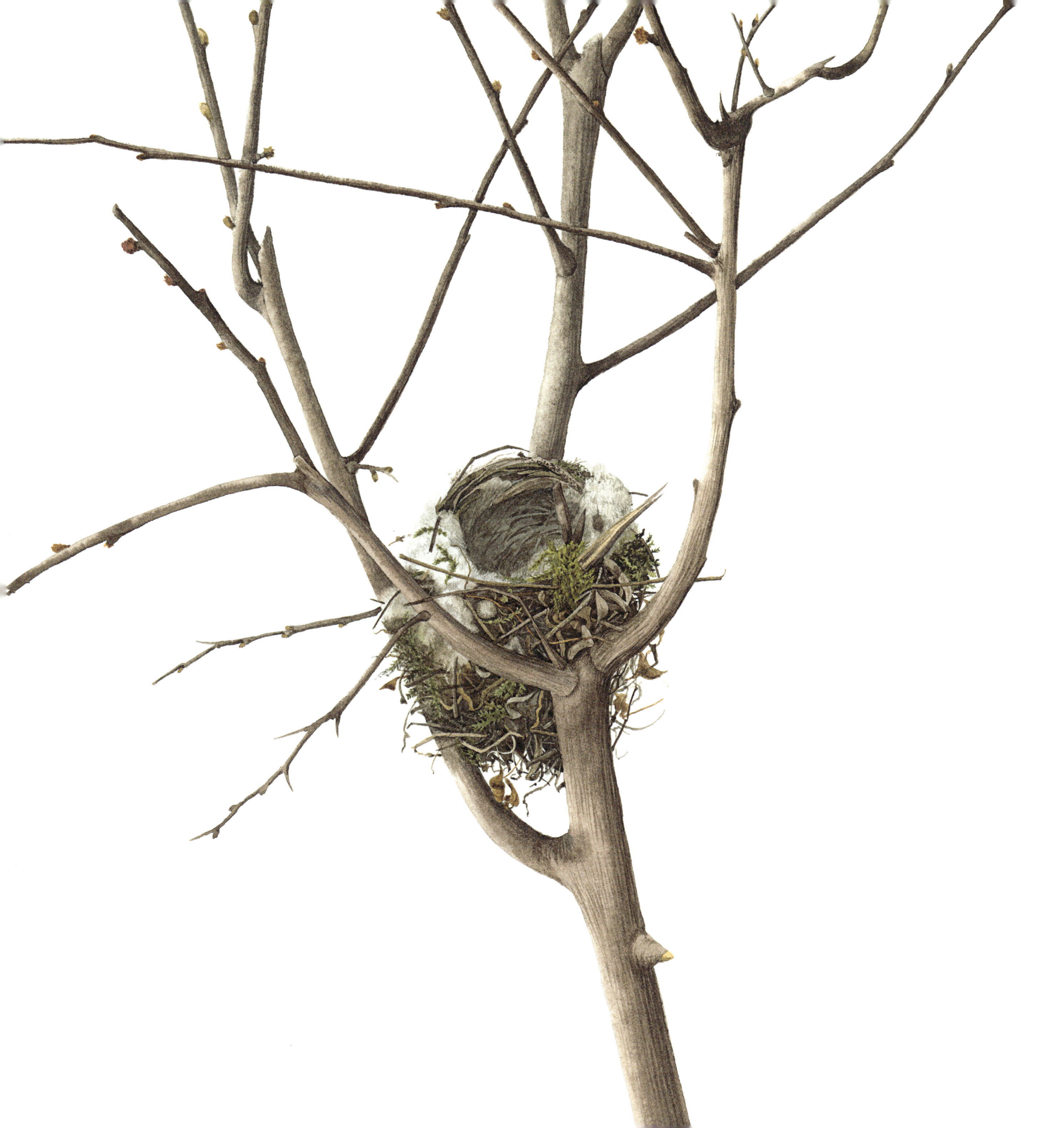

DUNNOCK

Prunella modularis

With this dunnock nest away from its twiggy position, you can see the construction more clearly. It has been built with grasses and a few fine twigs, and well lined with soft moss.

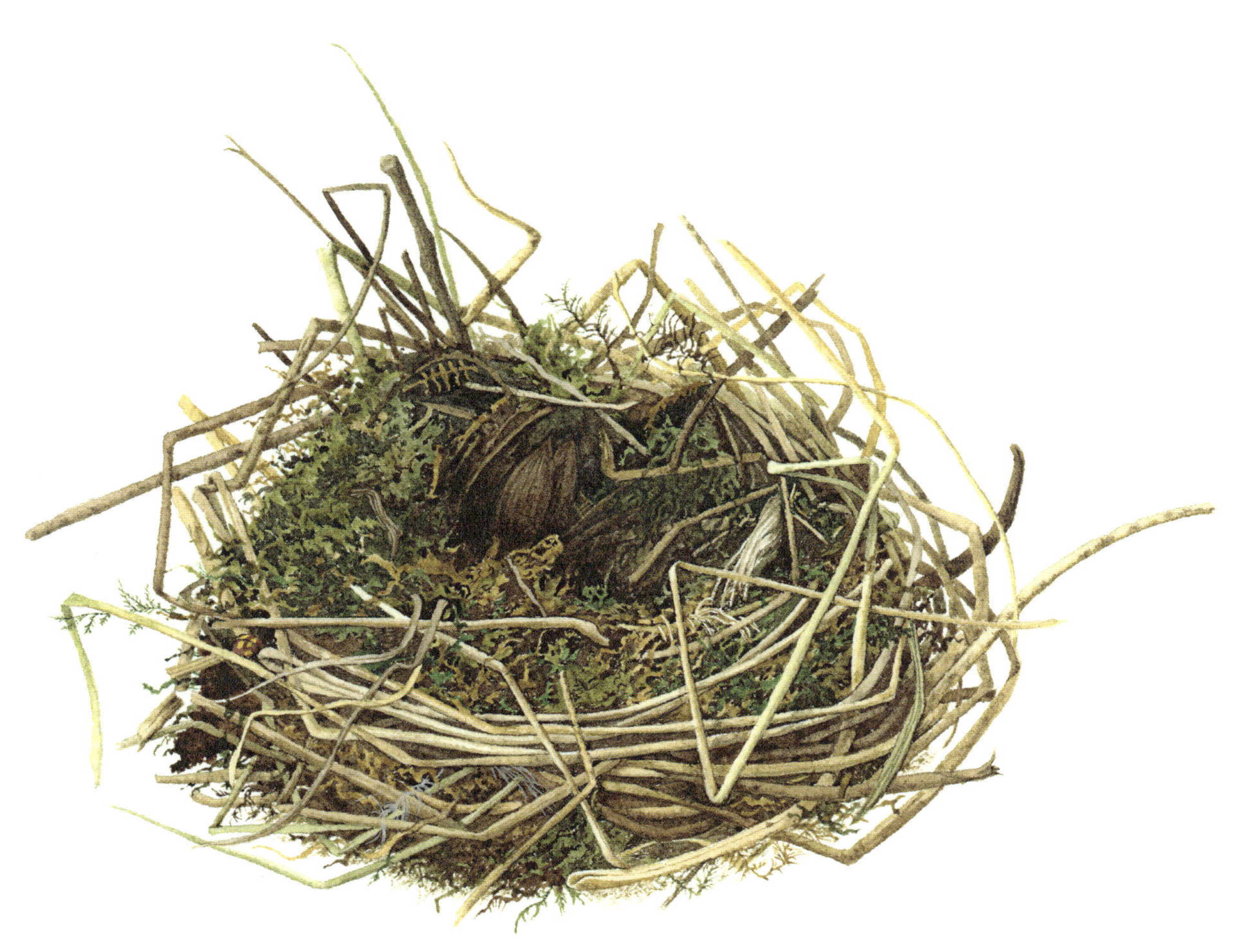

ROBIN

Erithacus rubecula

Resident	
Lifespan	About 5 years, although 8 years has been recorded
Diet	Worms, insects in summer, seeds, grain, berries in winter
Breeding season	March to June
Broods	2–3 clutches of 4–7 eggs
Position	In crevices or hollows, or in man-made sites like sheds and barns
Materials	Leaves, moss, grass, fine twigs
Lining	Fine grass, roots, hair, very occasionally feathers

Everyone knows the robin – a cheerful little bird who readily becomes tame. One summer we had one who joined in any meal taken in the garden, hopping around on the table between us, stealing crumbs. They defend their territory firmly and choose to build their nests in hollows in banks or tree stumps, but have been known to use shelves in sheds, old flower pots or even the pockets of old coats hanging in barns.

This nest was built into the corner of a box, and you can see that the left-hand side is thin, as it was hard up against the wall. The female builds the nest and incubates her eggs for twelve to fifteen days, but both parents feed the young for around a fortnight. They can produce two or three clutches in a season, and the male will take over sole responsibility for feeding the young if their broods overlap.

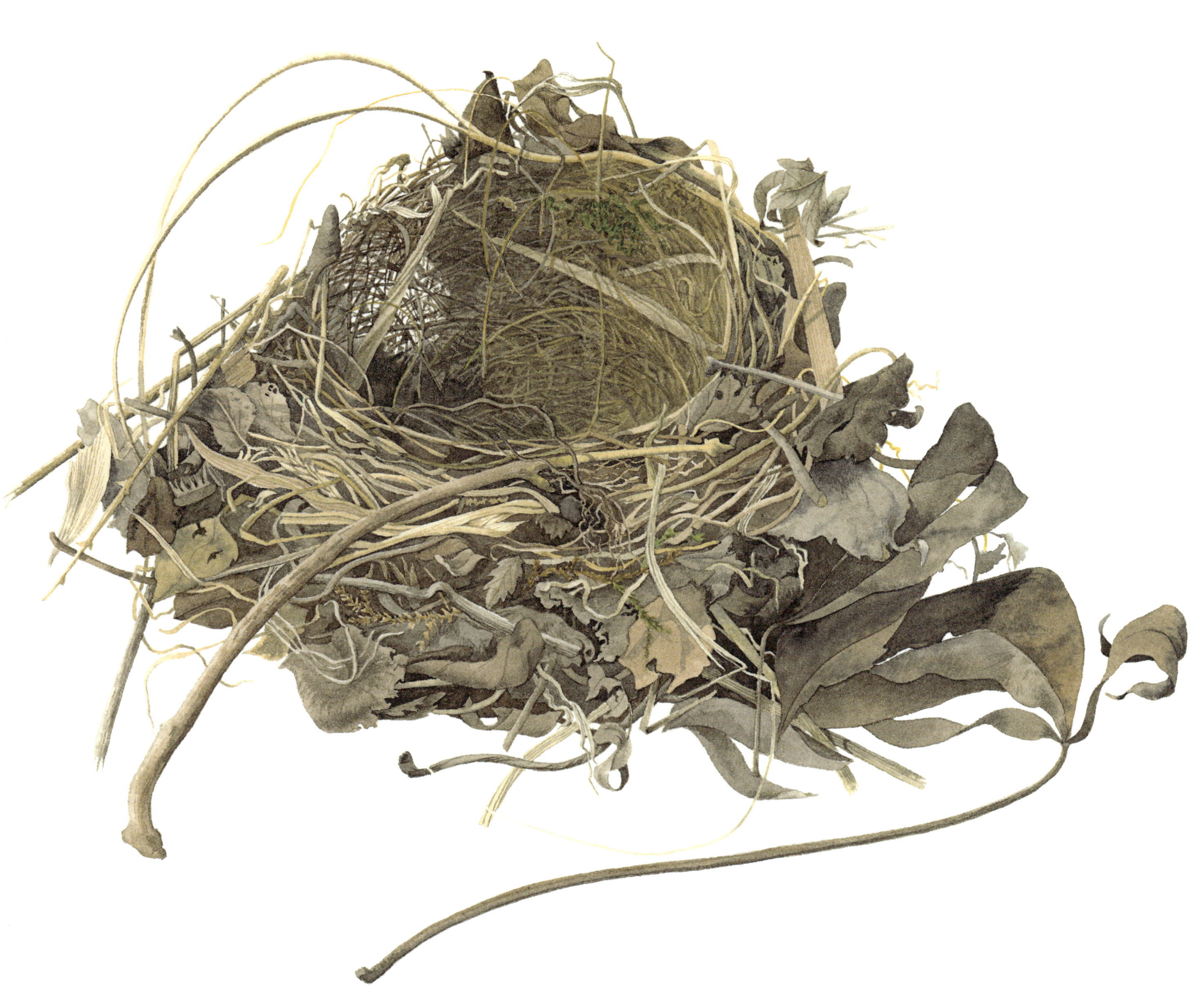

ROBIN

Erithacus rubecula

I was delighted by this nest when a friend produced it.
It is known that robins like to nest in old flower pots, but this
time a very smart rose pot had been used and (as my sister
pointed out) it even has lighting! Once again we can see
the robin's use of leaves in the nest's outer layer.

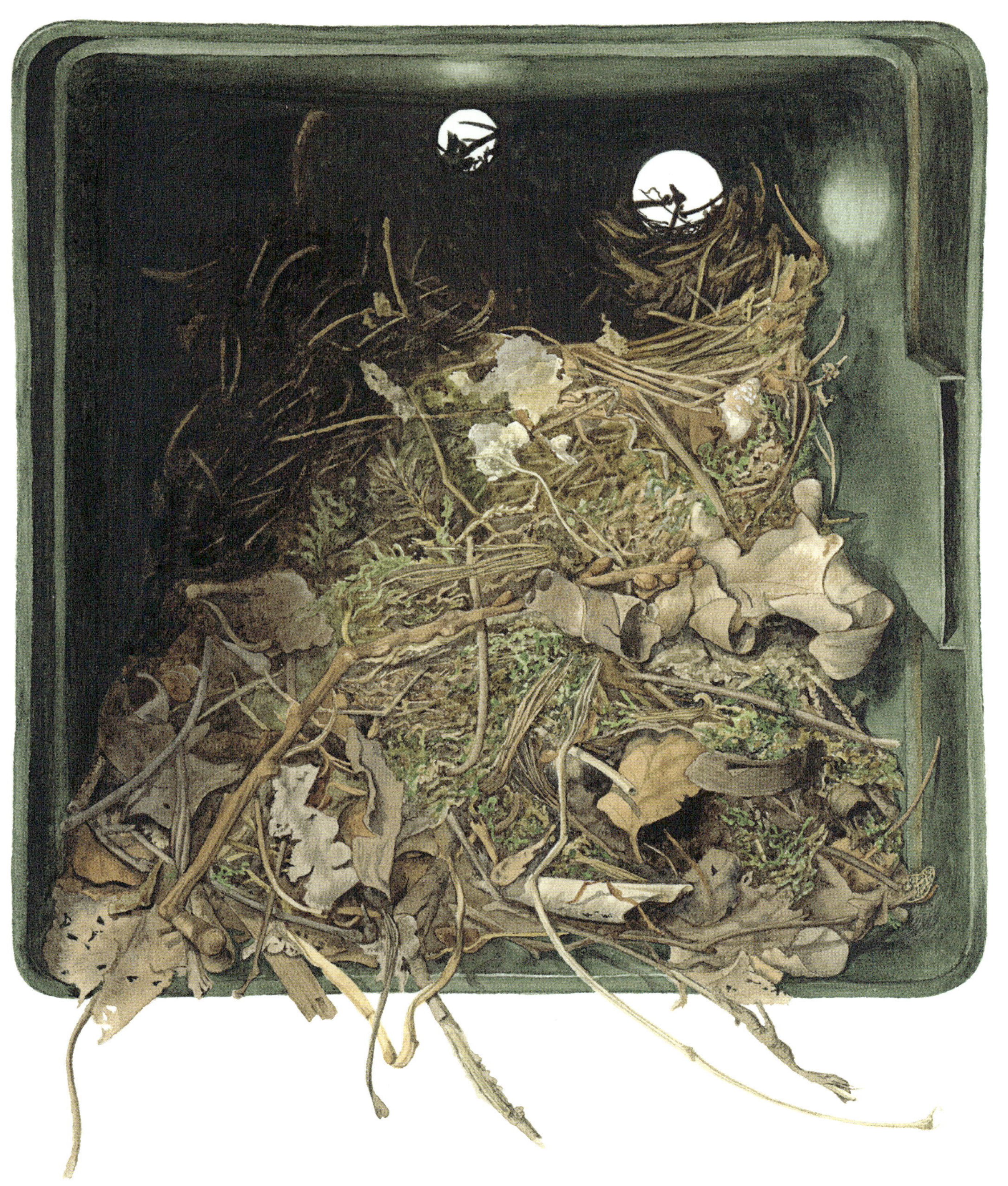

ROBIN

Erithacus rubecula

This very pretty nest shows a construction that is 'free standing' and not built within a box or other container. Once again the camouflage layer contains oak leaves, while a very pretty blue feather adds a final, decorative flourish.

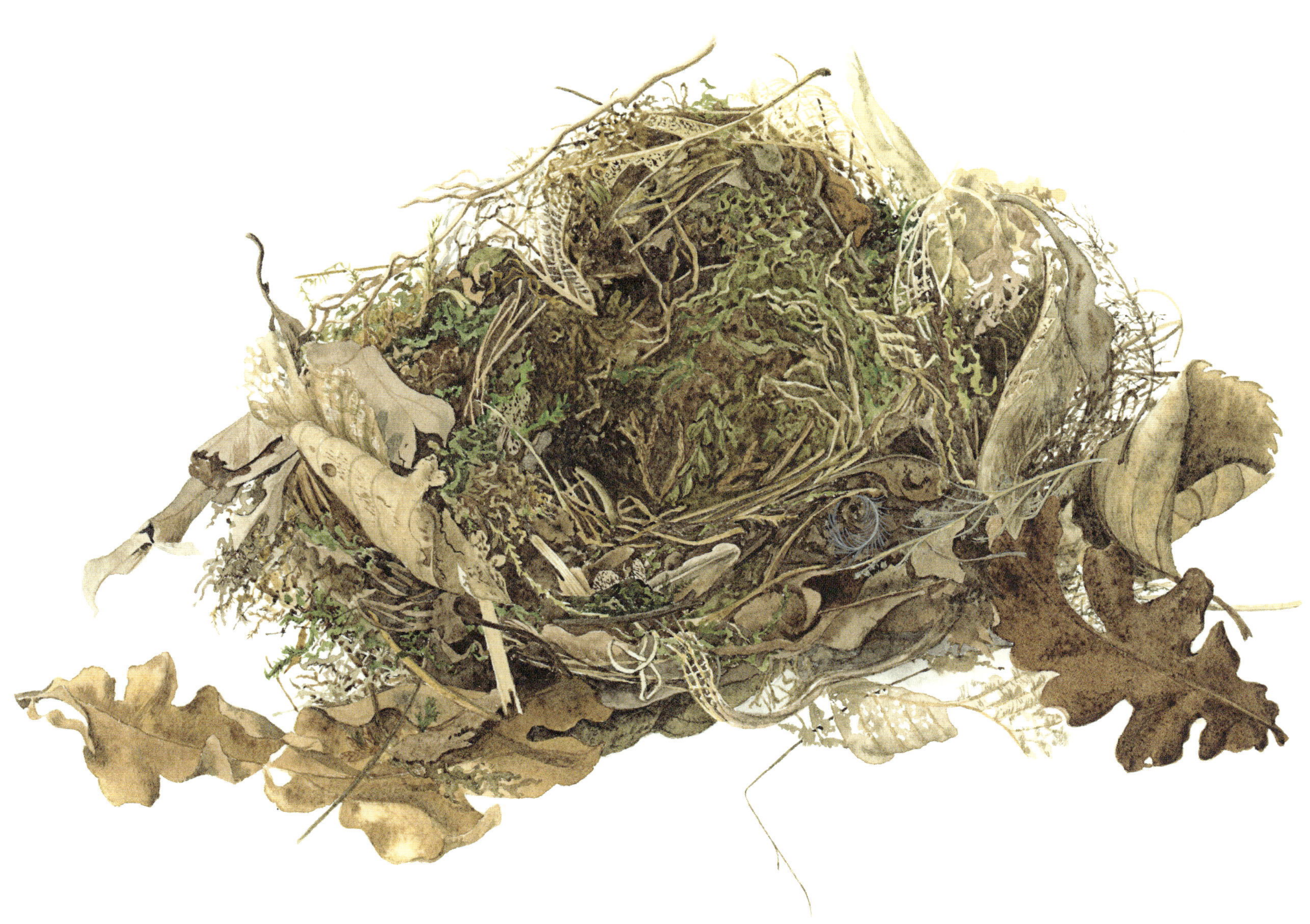

ROBIN

Erithacus rubecula

The identification of this nest baffled even Deon Warner.
The friend who found it – her dog having hauled it out of
a bush – had noticed some furious robins nearby and we
eventually concluded that it is probably an unfinished robin's
nest, its atypical use of local reeds being simply another
example of 'vernacular architecture'. Because it's unfinished,
there's no knowing how it would have been lined and whether
the end product might have been more recognizably a robin's
nest. At the beginning of this project I'd promised myself that
I would only paint nests that had been identified. This nest,
which demonstrates the skill with which birds weave together
plant materials, was the exception; it was so beautiful
I couldn't resist painting it as Deon and I went on puzzling
about its builder, before finally settling on the robin.

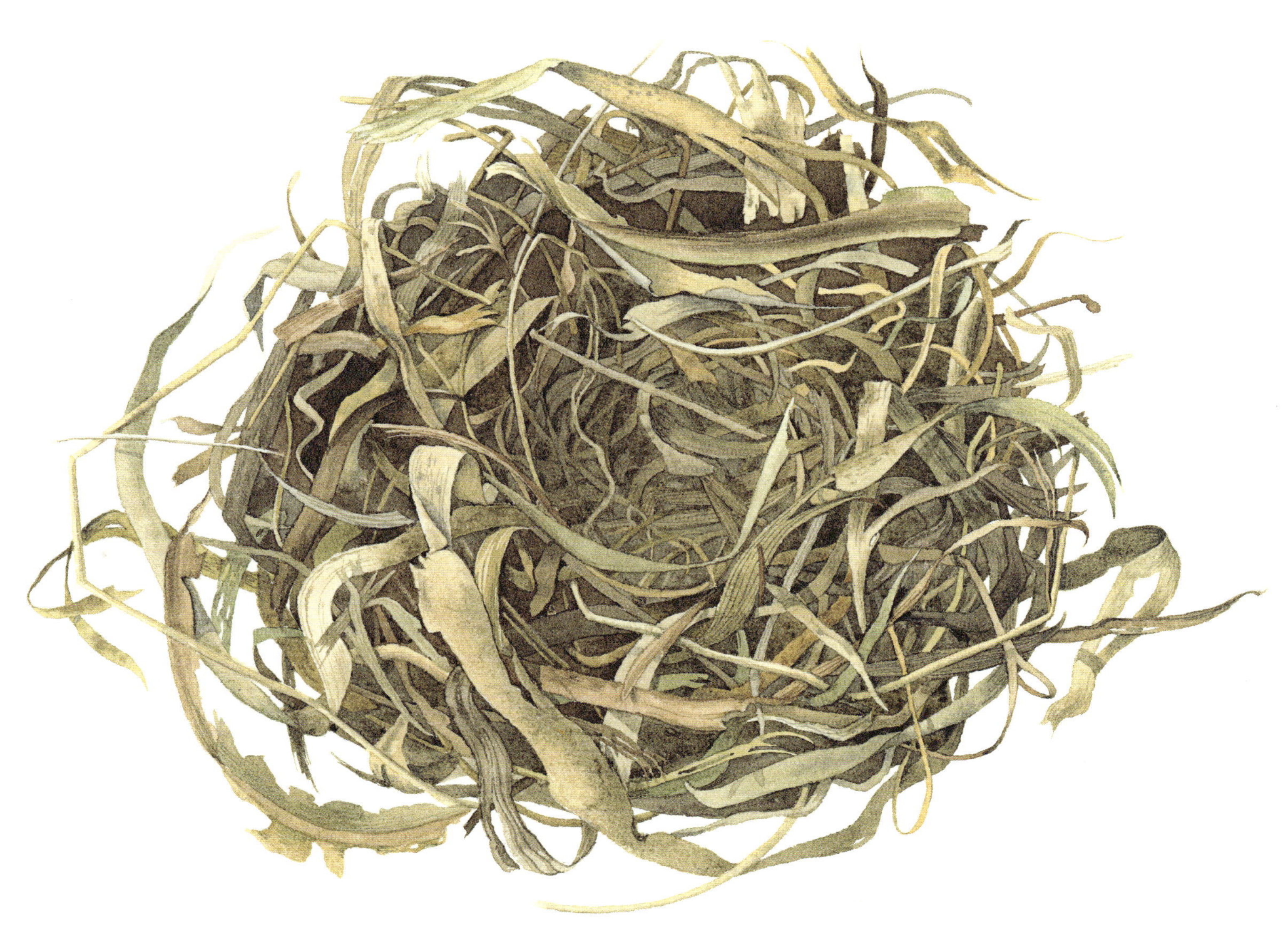

MISTLE THRUSH

Turdus viscivorus

Resident	
Lifespan	3–5 years, although 11 years has been recorded
Diet	Insects in summer; apples; berries, especially mistletoe and yew, in winter
Breeding season	February to May
Broods	1–2 clutches of 3–5 eggs
Position	Usually quite high in a forked branch of a tree or in open barns and sheds
Materials	Fine grasses, stems, twigs, an inner core of mud
Lining	Fine grasses

The name of the mistle thrush is thought to derive from a favourite food of this bird, which is responsible for much of mistletoe's spread through excretion, and also from wiping the plant's sticky juices off its beak onto tree branches. It is also known as the missel thrush, storm cock and mistletoe thrush, among other local names.

Mistle thrushes are early nesters, starting to build in February and rearing one or two broods. The nests are built by the female, usually in trees and at varying heights. They are bulky, untidy structures of fine grasses, stems and twigs, cemented by an inner core of mud, and are fearlessly defended by the adult birds. Incubation of twelve to fifteen days starts on completion of the clutch, and the young are tended by both parents for twelve to sixteen days before they fly at twenty days.

This wonderful nest was found on a rafter in a small, open-fronted brick shed belonging to neighbours. Once we were sure it was no longer in use we went to collect it, and found the remains of several more mistle thrush nests, suggesting that it is a site used year after year. I'd long been looking for such a nest, mostly in trees on the Isle of Arran, where I often see mistle thrushes, and here was a shedful in the Somerset village where I live. I have since learned that such open barns are also a common habitat. It's a marvellously built nest, and was a great pleasure – if a challenging one – to paint.

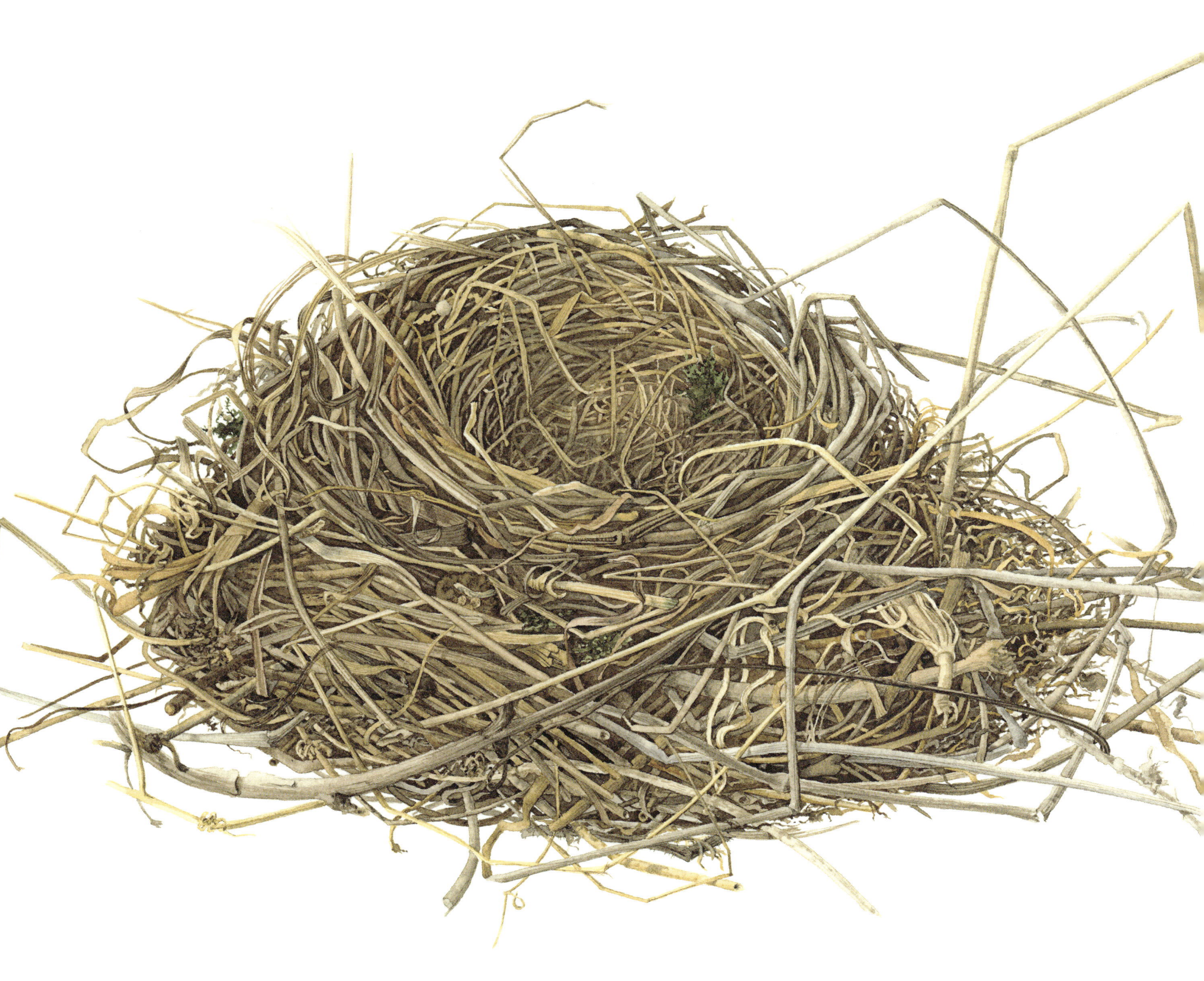

MISTLE THRUSH

Turdus viscivorus

Here's another example of the beautiful and intricate architecture of the mistle thrush. It was found in a tall shrub, and is remarkably similar to the one on the previous page.

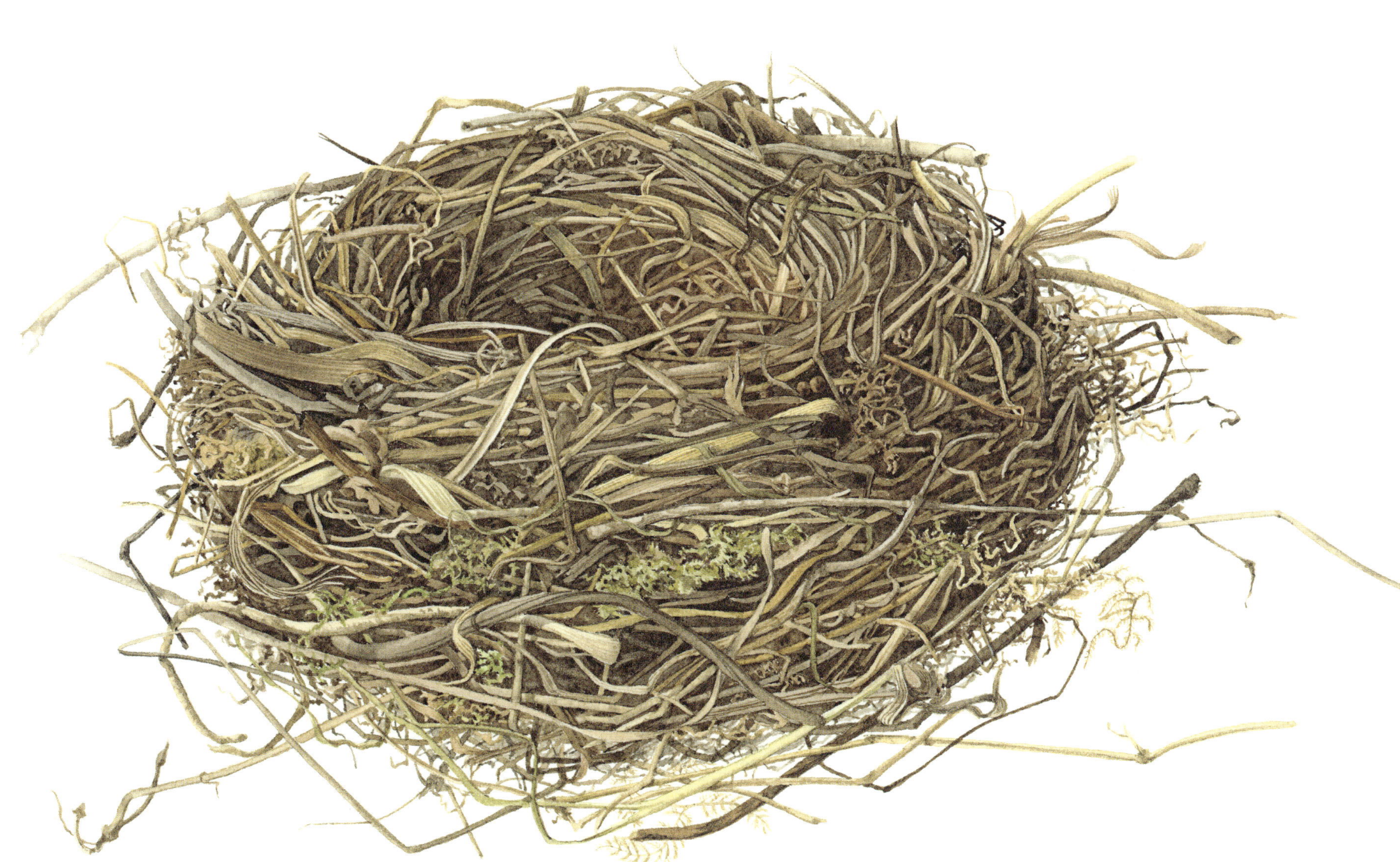

BLACKBIRD

Turdus merula

Resident	
Lifespan	About 5 years
Diet	Insects, worms, berries, apples, fruit
Breeding season	April to July
Broods	2–4 clutches of 3–5 eggs
Position	In thick bushes, forks of trees, among ivy, etc.
Materials	Twigs, moss, grass, roots, strips of bark, stuck together with mud
Lining	Fine grasses

The blackbird, famed for its song, is a familiar sight throughout Britain; although principally a woodland species, it adapts readily to gardens and parks.

A blackbird's nest is strong and heavy, a robust structure of twigs, grass, roots and moss, all firmly cemented with mud. It is largely the female who builds it, and she will use whatever she can find, including strips of wood and bits of rubbish – this nest includes bits of the red cedar from the hedge in which it was made – before lining it with fine grasses. She produces two or three clutches per season, generally building a new nest for each brood, although she will sometimes recycle some of the materials from the old nest for the new.

Incubation is mostly done by the female and lasts for eleven to seventeen days. Both adults feed the young in the nest until they fledge at about twelve to fourteen days. At this point each adult takes care of a group of the fledglings until they are ready to strike out on their own, usually after about three weeks. The female sometimes leaves her charges earlier than the male in order to prepare for the next brood.

My eldest grandson, Tom, found this nest in his den.

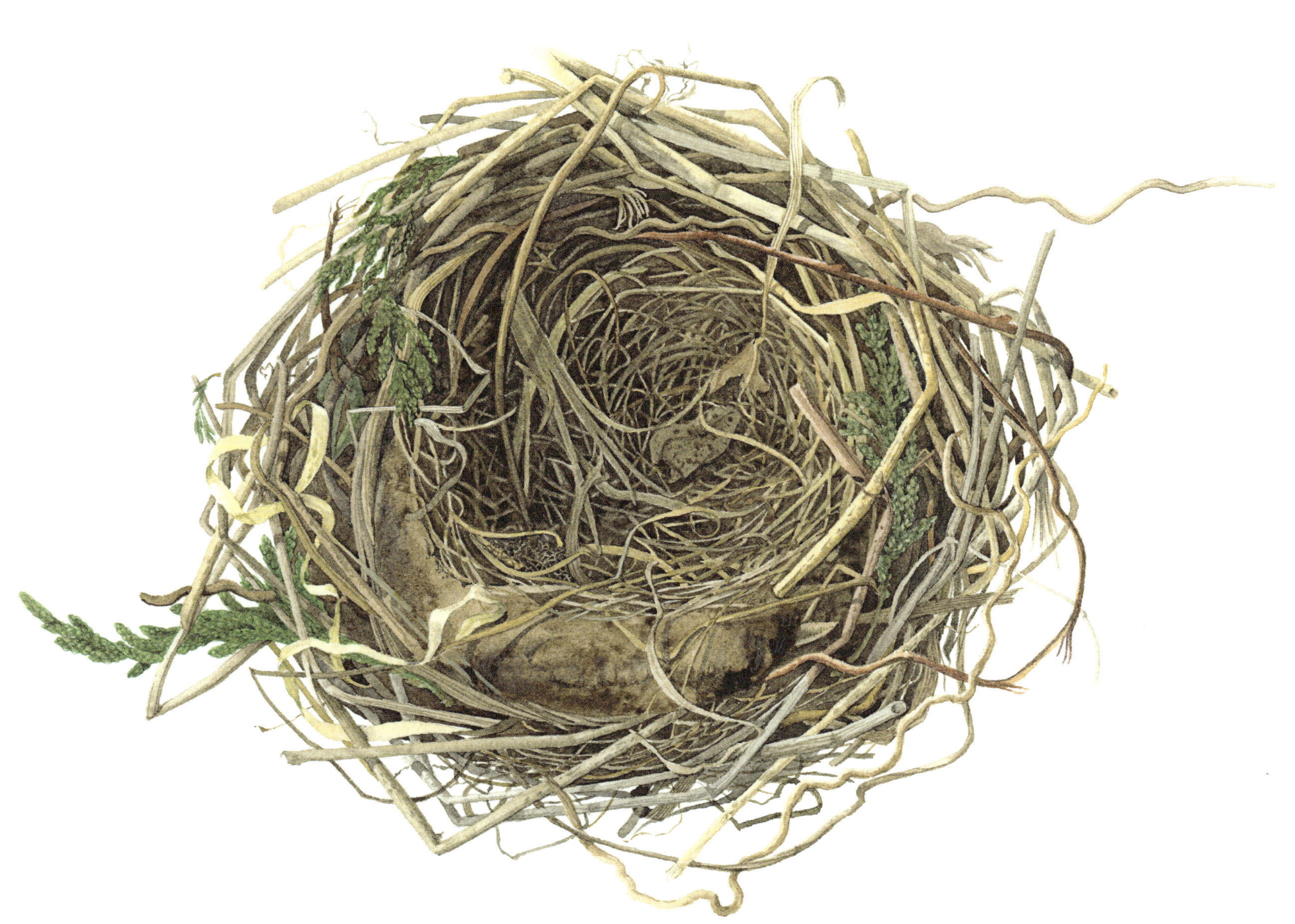

BLACKBIRD

Turdus merula

This very beautiful nest was found lying in the lane after
a storm. It has exactly the structure one would expect of
a blackbird's nest and includes the strips of wood or bark they
seem to favour as a binding, cemented by mud. As I painted it,
I marvelled at the strength the bird must have employed
to manoeuvre these materials into position. The final nest
is robust and sits heavily in the hand.

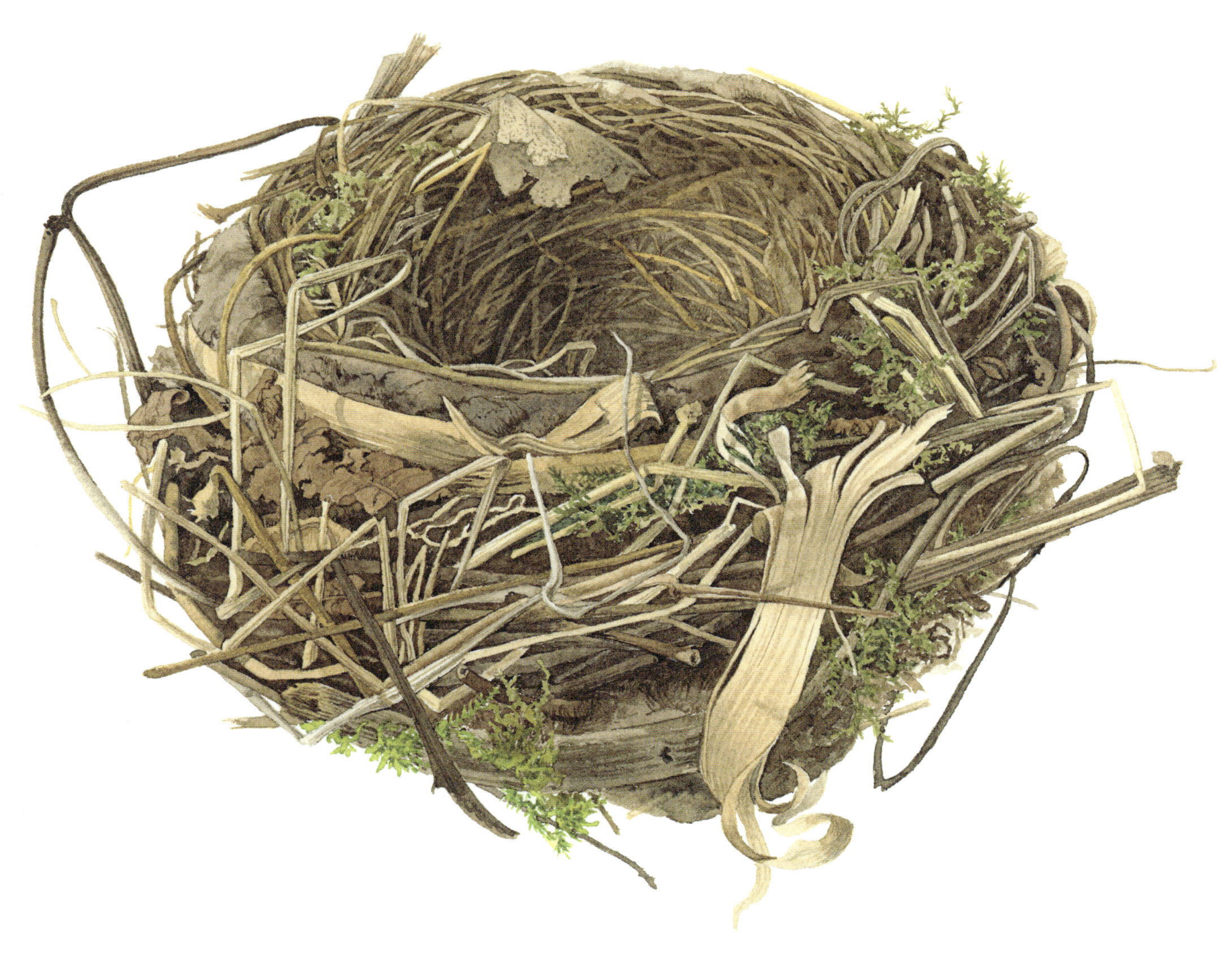

BLACKBIRD

Turdus merula

One wild, stormy January evening a friend brought me this
nest in a very smart shoebox. Having been out since the
previous spring it was completely sodden and beginning to
disintegrate. We were delighted by its little crop of weeds –
groundsel, celandine and grass – presumably sprouted from
seeds buried in the mud which cements the nest together.
It also incorporates a food label tucked into the mud –
an example of a blackbird making use of available materials.

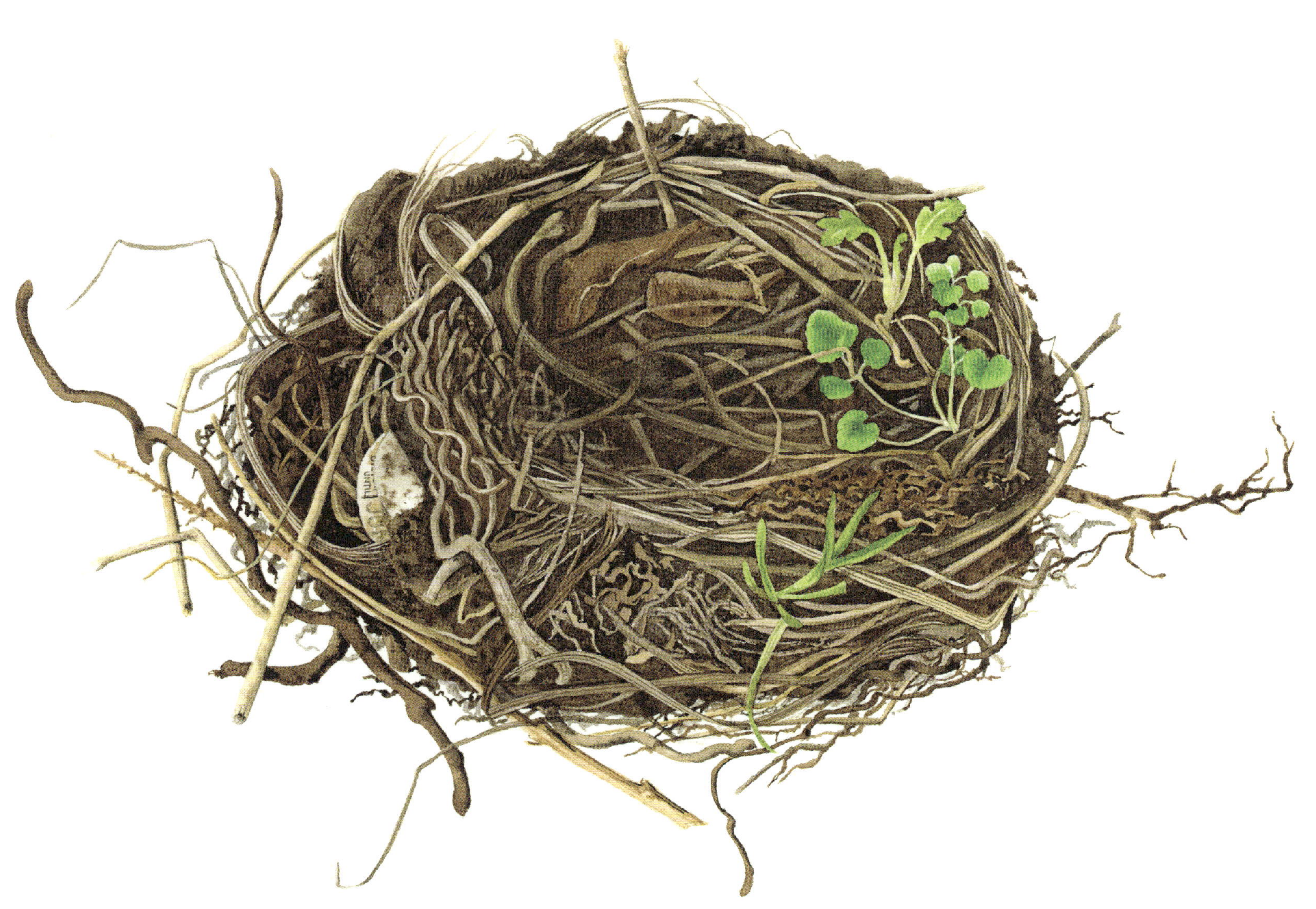

BLACKBIRD
Turdus merula

This blackbird's nest includes rubbish throughout, with pieces of plastic sacking in the camouflage layer and polythene among the grasses in the lining. It makes a fascinating nest, but also serves as a reminder that our use of plastic is spreading much too far into the animal kingdom. The nest was found by Utta Brown, who was already a heroine in this project, as it was she who introduced me to Deon Warner.

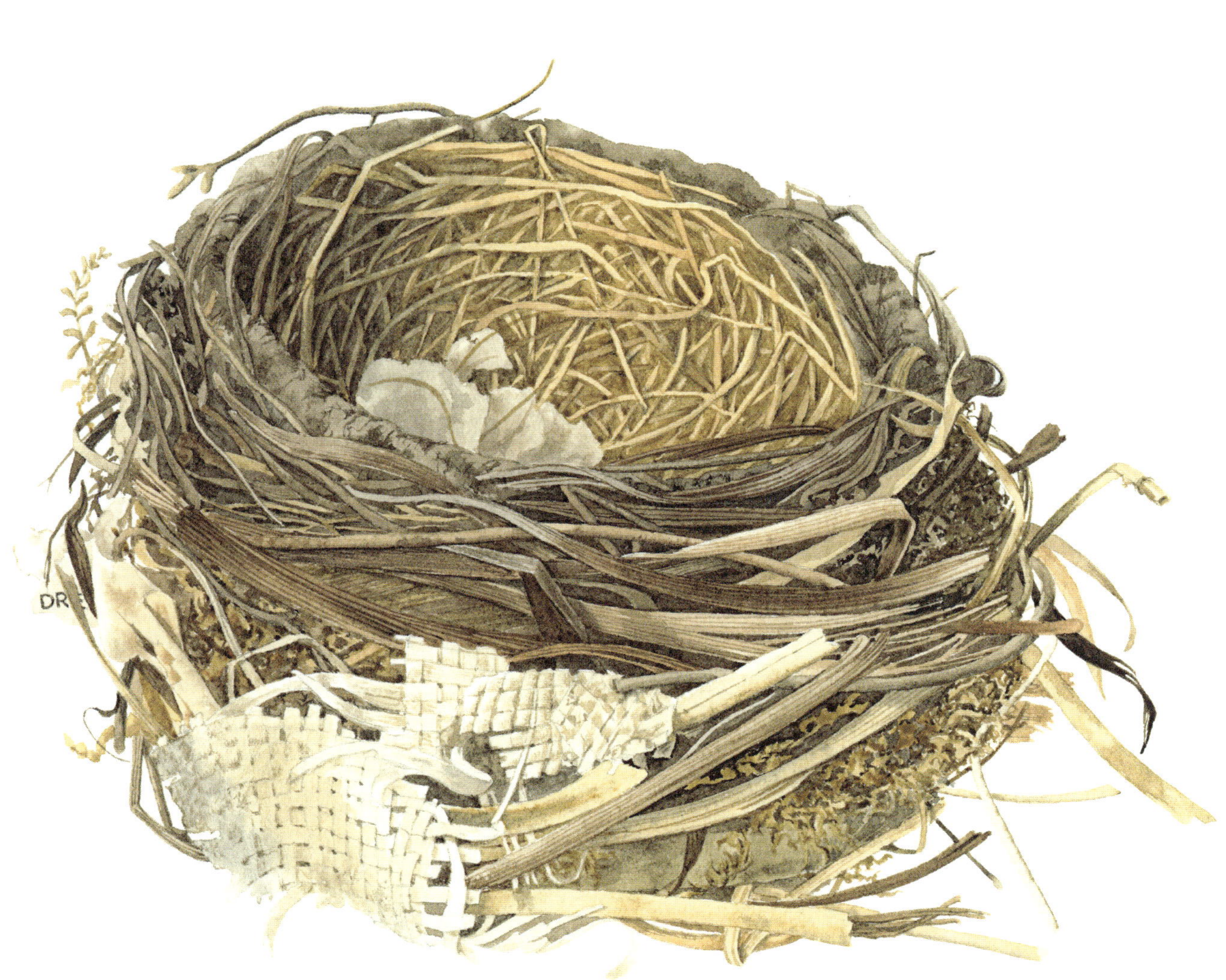

SONG THRUSH
Turdus philomelos

Resident	Sometimes migrates from northern to southern Britain in winter
Lifespan	5–10 years, although 13 years has been recorded
Diet	Worms, caterpillars, snails, berries in winter
Breeding season	March to July
Broods	1–4 clutches of 3–5 eggs
Position	In dense shrubs or conifers on woodland edges, or from 1–4 metres up in ivy- or honeysuckle-covered trees
Materials	Mud, twigs, moss, leaves, grasses
Lining	Mud, wood pulp made with saliva and rotten wood

Widely admired for its song and its unique ability to crack snail shells, the song thrush also deserves praise for its nest, which is typically a sturdy structure cemented with mud and smoothly lined. It is usually positioned quite low down, but well hidden, in dense shrubs on woodland edges. The female builds the nest, smoothing the lining of mud and wood pulp into an immaculate cup with her breast, and does most of the incubation of the eggs, for eleven to fifteen days, before both parents feed the young for their twelve to sixteen days in the nest. There is sometimes a second brood, even a third or fourth in the southernmost range of its habitat.

My sister found this nest after a storm while we were clearing a fallen mulberry tree at our father's house. It was newly made and included a long, fresh stem of grass which, sadly, had dried by the time I came to paint it.

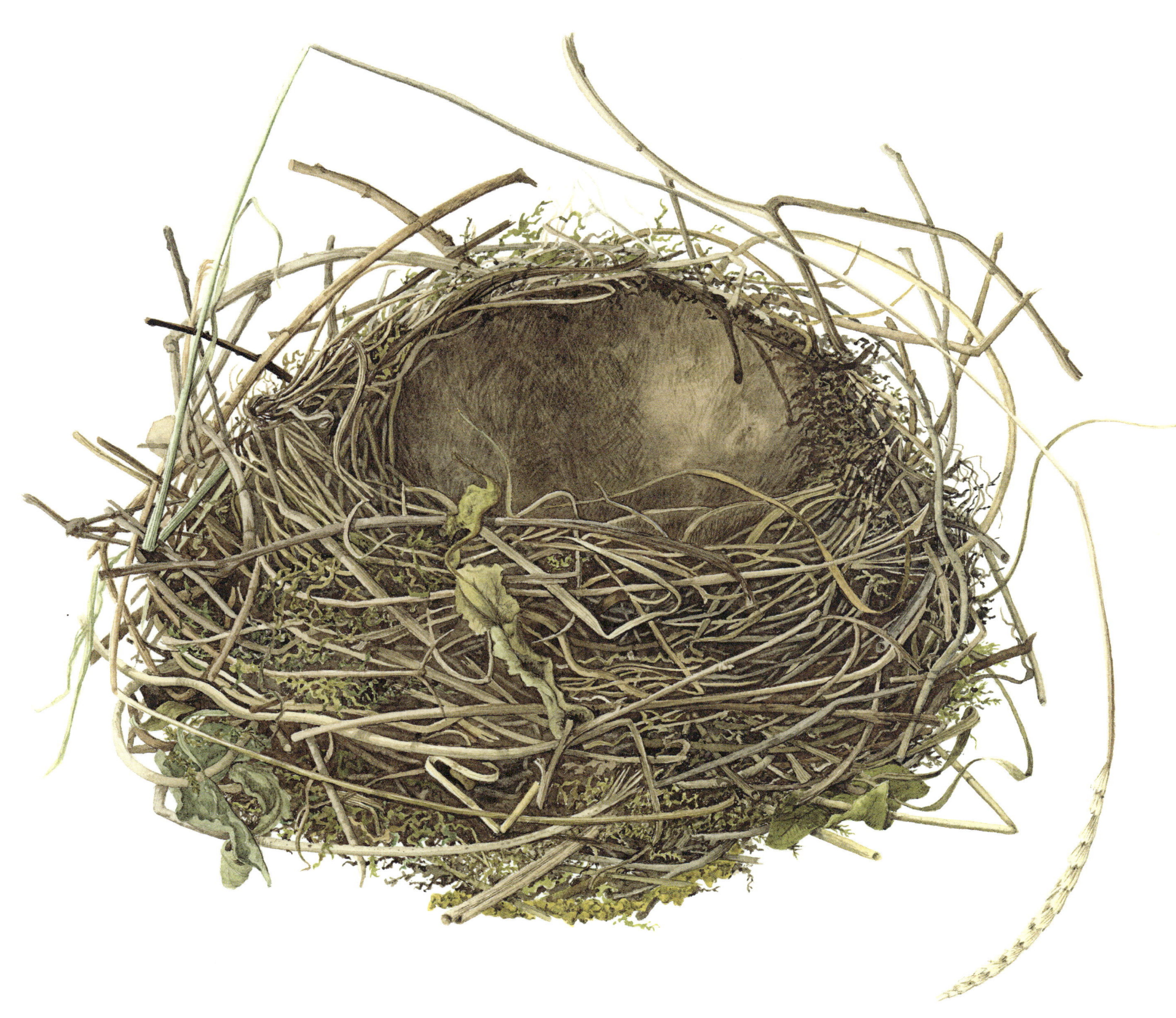

SONG THRUSH

Turdus philomelos

This nest shows how the architecture of the song thrush
is remarkably consistent. The example on the previous page
was found in East Anglia, in a fallen tree, while this one was
found in Somerset in brambles. Both nests are easily recognized
by their immaculate linings of wood pulp within twiggy
frameworks that also contain leaves and moss.

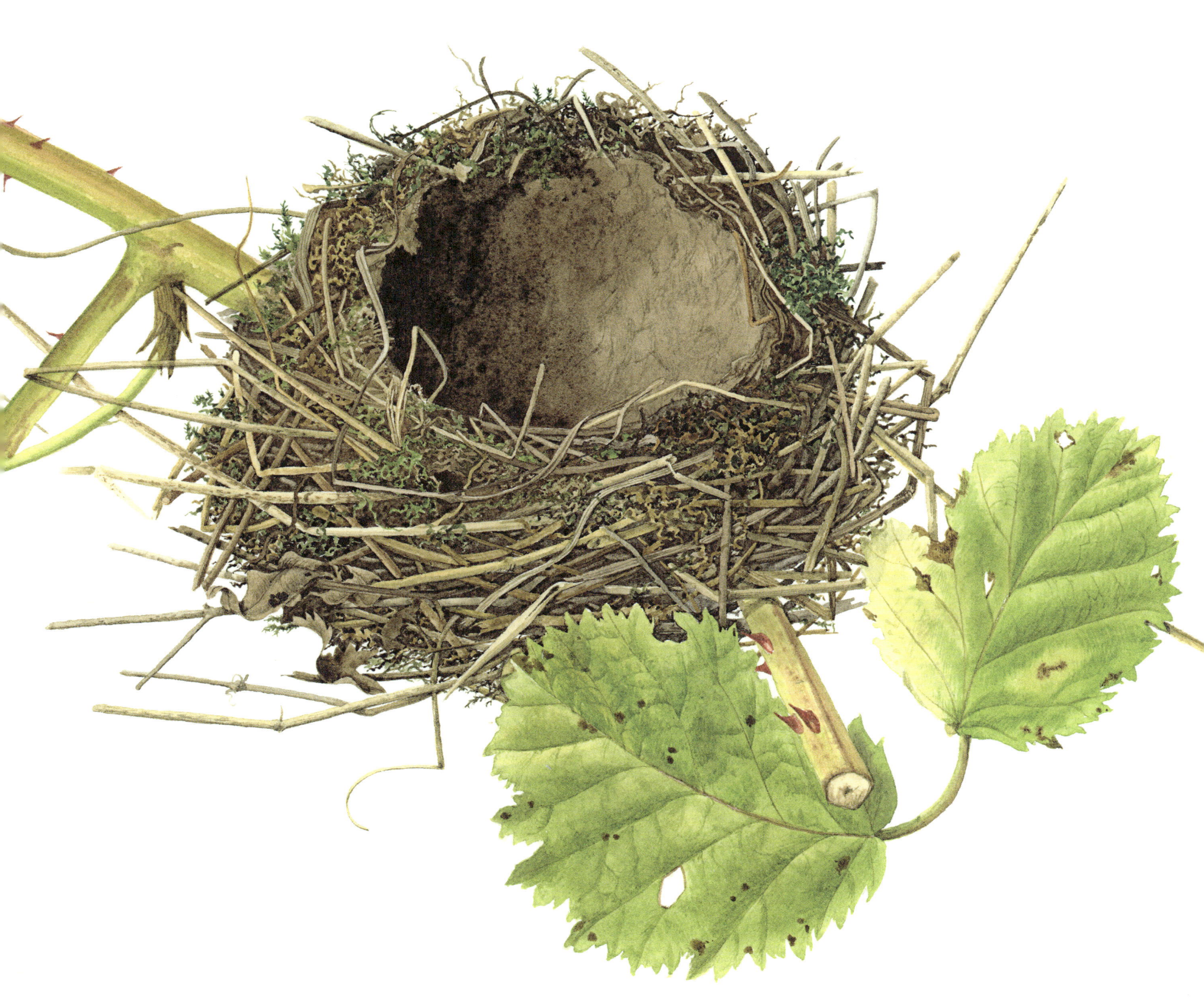

SONG THRUSH

Turdus philomelos

This song thrush nest was found in Scotland, on the Isle of Arran, when it fell out of a clematis onto the wood pile below. It is made with a very liberal layer of moss as camouflage, and shows clearly how song thrushes line their nests with wood pulp. The nest was soaked by the rain, which had washed away any mud and dust to reveal a firm, clean lining, almost like modern chip board.

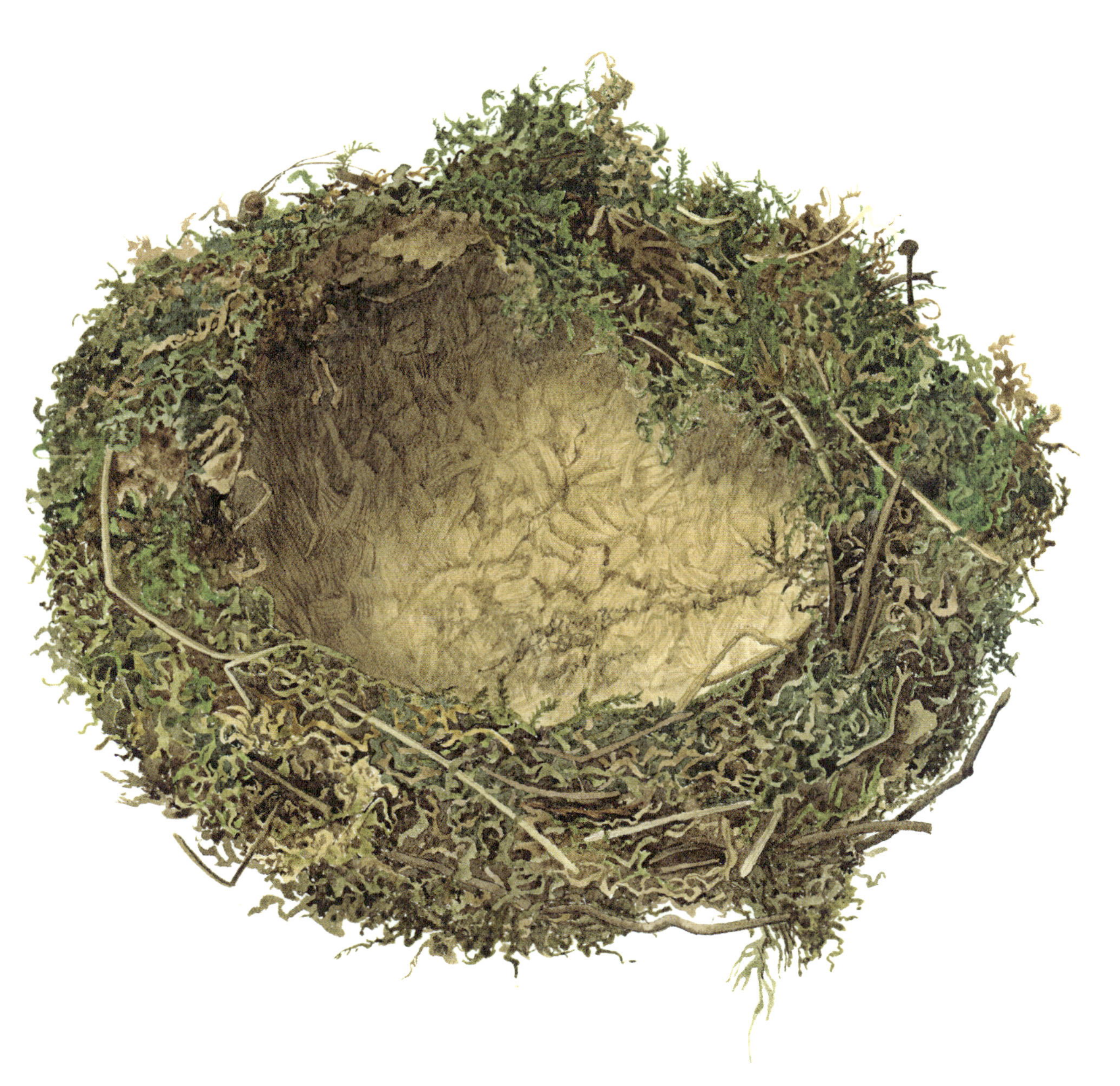

REED WARBLER

Acrocephalus scirpaceus

Migrant	Arrives in April and May from Europe and Africa
Lifespan	About 5 years, although 12 years has been recorded
Diet	Insects
Breeding season	May to July
Broods	1–2 clutches of 3–6 eggs
Position	Reed beds in water; in vegetation on banks of waterways
Materials	Grasses, cobwebs, moss, rootlets
Lining	Plant down, hair, feathers

The reed warbler is a migrant that winters in Africa and reaches Britain in late spring, starting its nest building in late May. The nest is built by both male and female, although the female does the lion's share. A deep cup is formed from grasses, pieces of reed, moss and cobwebs, cleverly suspended between three to five reeds. It takes four days to build the structure and another three to line it. As the season progresses the reeds continue to grow, raising the nest ever higher above the water level. Both adults incubate the eggs for eleven to twelve days, and share the feeding of the young for the thirteen days they remain in the nest. They may produce a second brood. The reed warbler nest is one favoured by cuckoos.

My sister and I found this nest in our father's study when we cleared it after his death. His garden was on the banks of the River Stour and he probably found it there. He went on tackling everything long after the age when most people have taken to a quieter life, and our sad task was relieved by the happy thought of our father, well into his nineties, clambering down the bank to retrieve this nest.

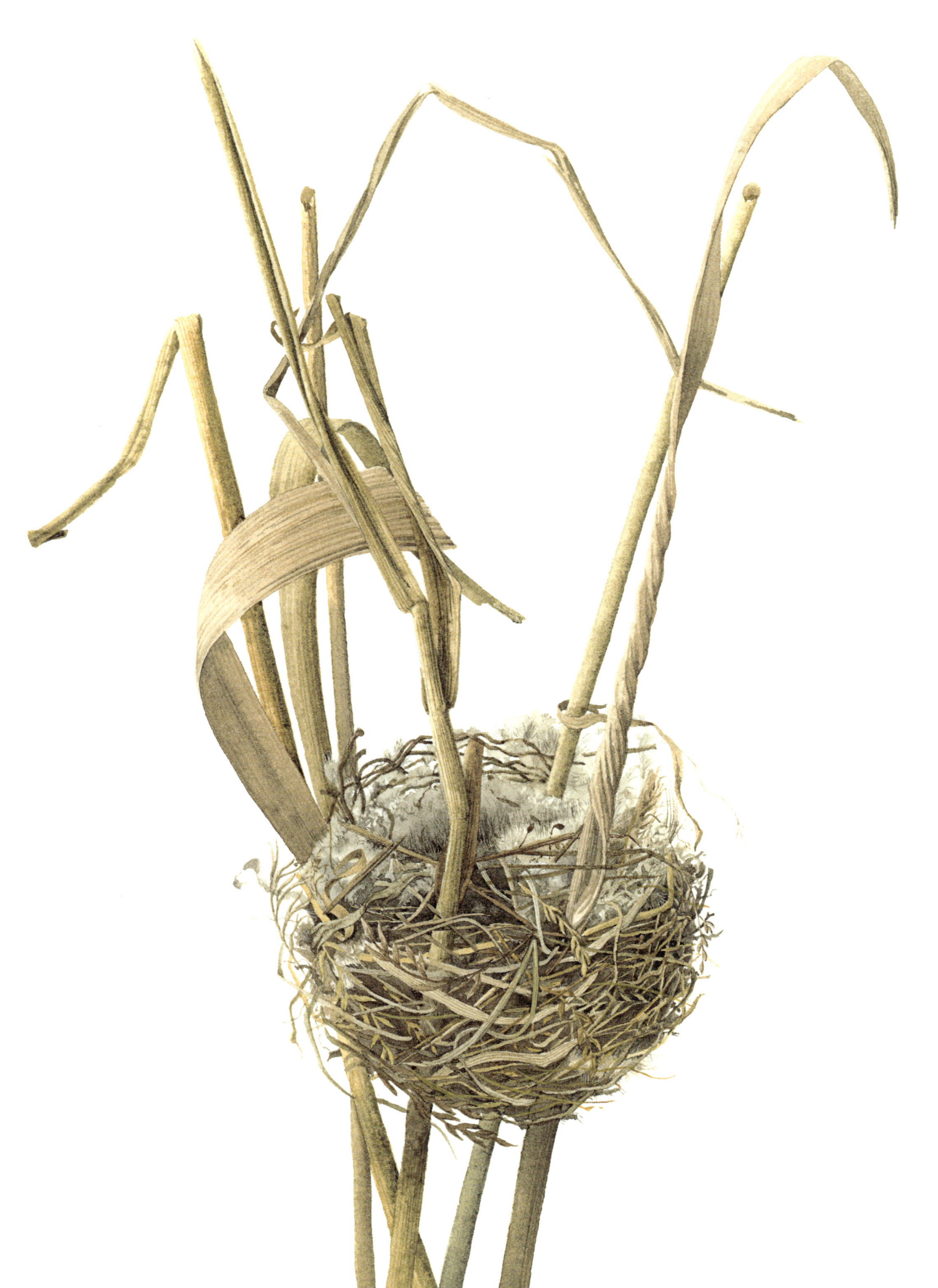

CHIFFCHAFF

Phylloscopus collybita

Migrant	Most head south in winter to the Mediterranean and North Africa
Lifespan	Up to 5 years
Diet	Mainly insects such as midges, flies, moth caterpillars; occasionally seeds and berries
Breeding season	April to June
Broods	1–2 clutches of 5–6 eggs
Position	In dense vegetation on or near ground
Materials	Grass, moss, leaves, fern fronds, cobwebs
Lining	Feathers, hair

The chiffchaff, a small bird about the same size as a blue tit, is a partial migrant, with relatively few remaining in the south of Britain all year round. Most fly south towards the end of September, returning in March and April to breed in Britain and elsewhere in northern Europe.

The chiffchaff nest is often described as 'oven shaped'; it is domed and tapers towards the back, with a side entrance. It is built by the female, low in dense undergrowth. She then lays her eggs, incubates them for thirteen to fifteen days and does most of the feeding of the nestlings, which fledge at about twelve to fifteen days. The care for the fledglings continues for another ten to nineteen days and is shared by the parents.

During the early stages of this project, Deon Warner promised himself he would find me a chiffchaff nest. About three years later he rang up in triumph to say he'd got it.

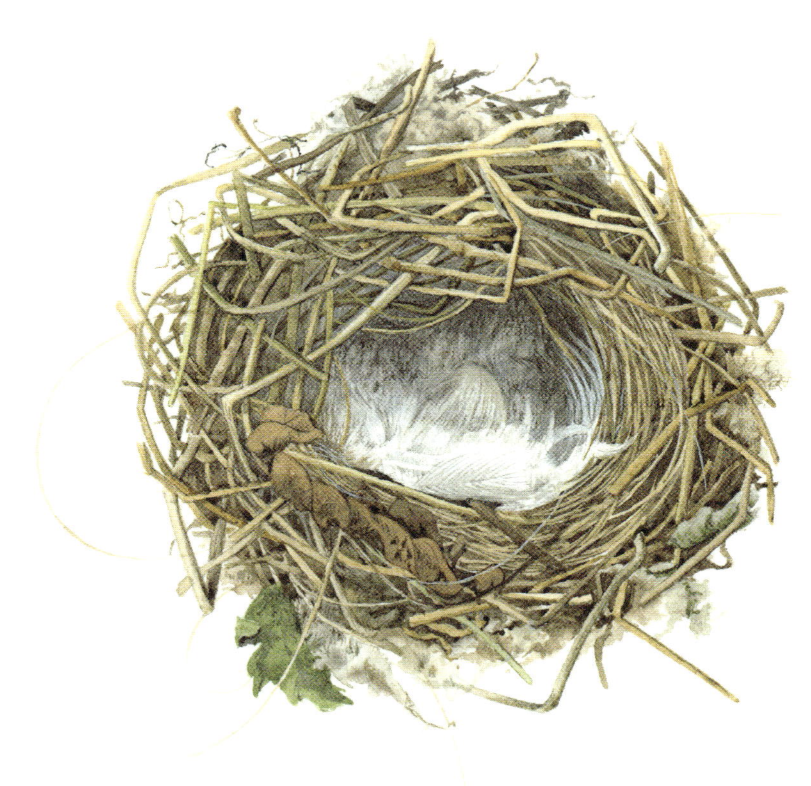

CHIFFCHAFF

Phylloscopus collybita

I spent most of 2020, when the world was gripped by the coronavirus pandemic, working on this book. England was blessed with a wonderful spring of warm weather and birdsong, and the 'lockdown' restrictions on human activity, imposed to curb the virus, provided me with a perfect opportunity to paint the last few nests I had waiting from previous seasons, while this year's nests were being built.

One morning a friend rang me with the news that she had come across a nest under her hedge. That evening my husband and I walked through fields of buttercups to collect it. I was delighted by the nest, which Belinda had placed on top of her gate for me to collect, mindful of the 'social distancing' rules that forbade close contact. She pointed out where a trail of wood shavings showed how the nest had been pulled out of its position in a clump of hart's tongue fern, probably by a magpie. As we walked home, passing the basket between us when we climbed over stiles, the tragedy which had befallen both this nest and the world seemed very far away, and we felt most fortunate to be so peacefully cocooned in the depths of Somerset.

The liberal use of wood shavings on the outside of this chiffchaff nest makes it seem much bigger than the one on the previous page, but the inside dimensions are the same. Belinda searched for the source of the wood shavings without success, but the fact that this nest was raided by a predator suggests that they didn't provide the best camouflage for its situation among ferns under a hedge.

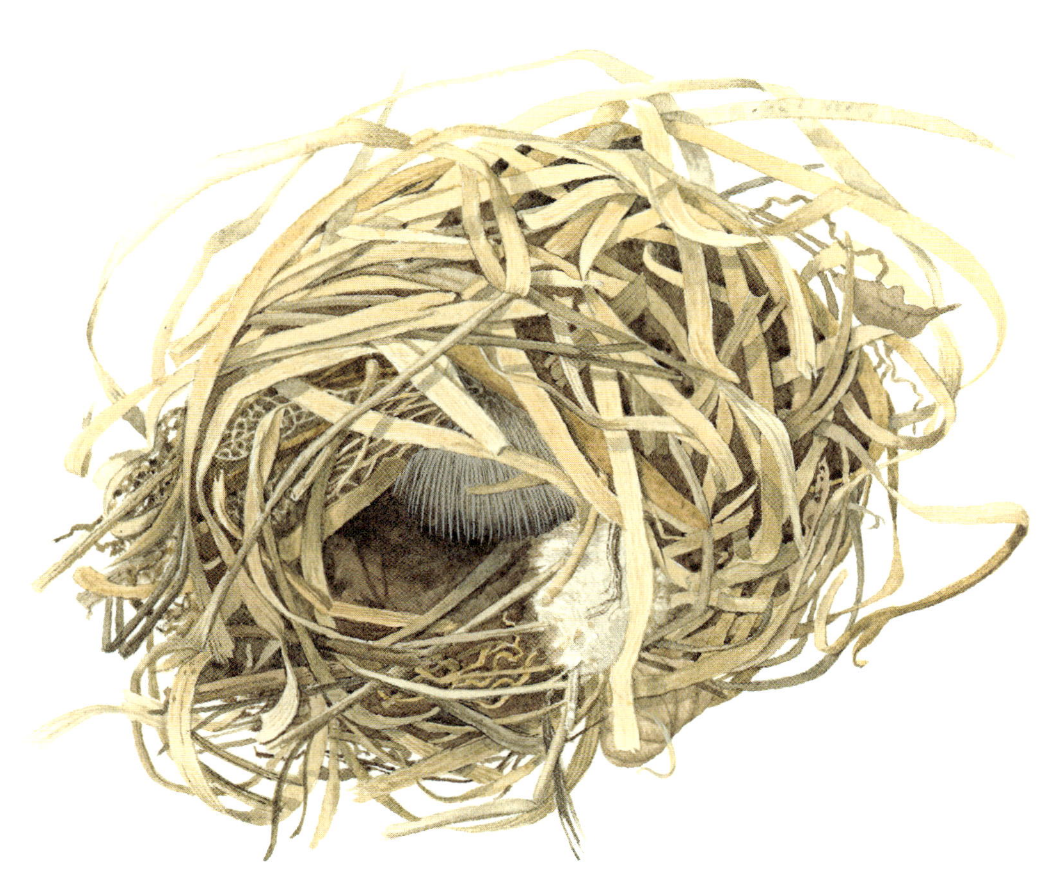

GOLDCREST

Regulus regulus

Resident

Lifespan — 2–3 years, although 7 years has been recorded

Diet — Insects including spiders, flies, small caterpillars and moth eggs; occasionally seeds

Breeding season — Late April to June

Broods — 1–2 clutches of up to 12 eggs

Position — Towards the end of a branch, often in conifer forests or yew trees

Materials — Small twigs, moss, lichen, grasses, feathers, held together by cobwebs

Lining — Feathers, hair

The goldcrest is Europe's smallest bird, weighing less than six grams, and is known for being a busy little bird, perpetually on the move. It is monogamous. Both male and female birds build the neat, deeply cupped nest near the end of a branch, often in conifer forests. This nest is beautifully constructed of small twigs, well-felted moss, lichen and cobwebs, and lined with feathers and hair. The hen lays up to twelve eggs – more than her body weight – and then incubates them diligently for fourteen to seventeen days. Both parents feed the young for nearly three weeks until they leave the nest, continuing to feed the fledglings for another two weeks until they are independent.

They may build a second nest and embark on another brood before the first has fledged, in which case the male continues the care of the first brood while the female incubates the second. Goldcrests are resident in Britain, but in winter the population may be increased by migrants from northern Europe. At this time of year goldcrests often flock together with other species, especially tits.

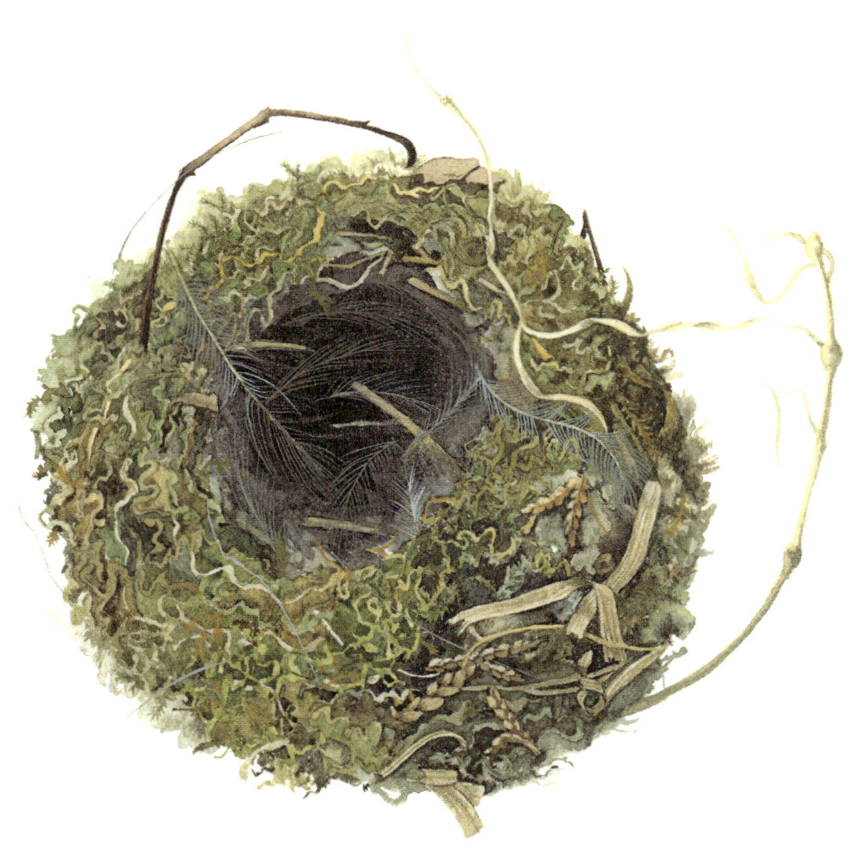

GOLDCREST
Regulus regulus

This nest probably started out looking like the one on the previous page, but it has clearly been well used and now shows the wear and tear of raising a family. It can be seen, from the needles inside the nest, that it was built in a yew tree, and the use of several pigeon feathers in its construction suggests that there were pigeons nesting nearby.

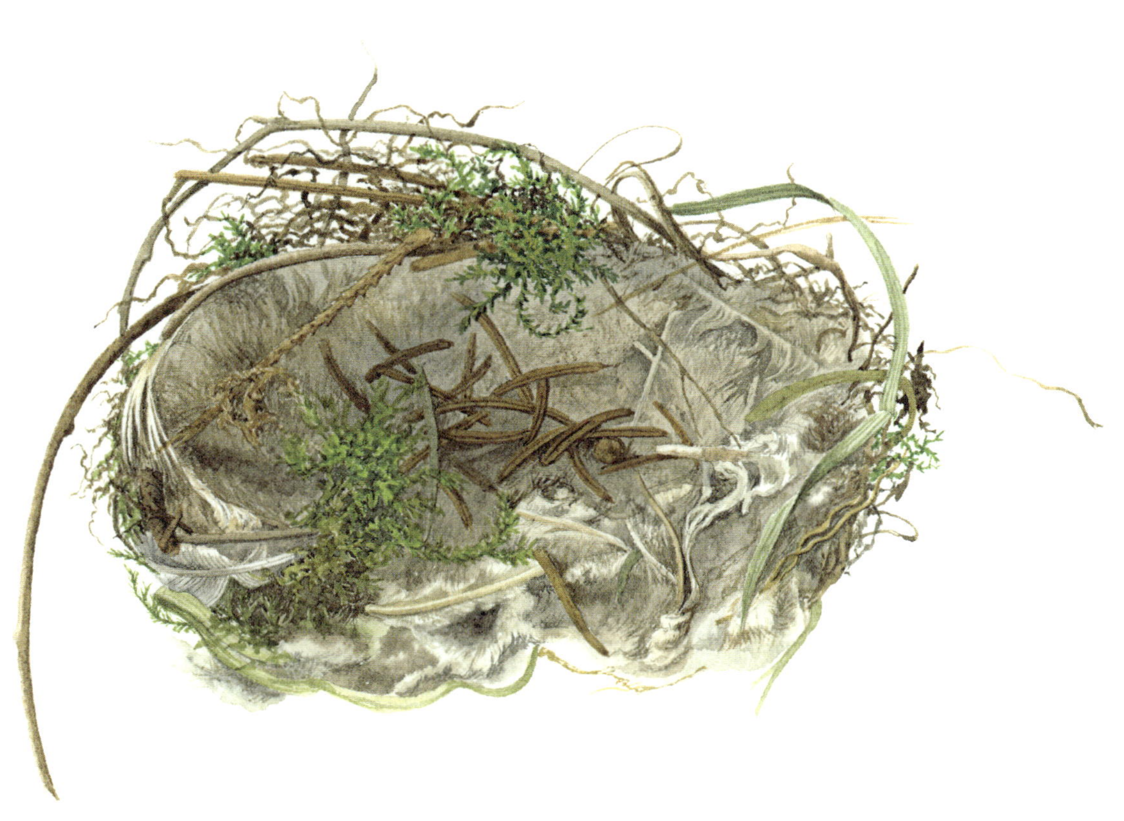

BLACKCAP

Sylvia atricapilla

Migrant	Northern populations migrate, southern ones are often resident
Lifespan	About 5 years, although 10 years has been recorded
Diet	Insects, caterpillars, berries
Breeding season	May to July
Broods	1–2 clutches of 4–6 eggs
Position	Low in hedges, bushes and brambles
Materials	Grasses, moss, rootlets, hair, sometimes mud or cobwebs
Lining	Feathers, moss, hair

The blackcap is a partial migrant, mostly wintering in southern Europe and North Africa, returning to these shores in mid-April. The cock bird is known for his song, which is fluting, melodic and varied and is generally acknowledged to be second only to the nightingale's. Indeed, in some parts of Britain the blackcap is known as the mock nightingale.

The male builds several nests, neat cups beautifully anchored into position, often in hawthorn or brambles, but he does not finish them. That is left to the female, who chooses her preferred nest and completes the rudimentary beginning by lining it with feathers, moss and hair. Both adults incubate the eggs for eleven to fourteen days, starting incubation with the second or third egg laid. They feed the young for ten to twelve days before they fledge. Some pairs will then have a second brood.

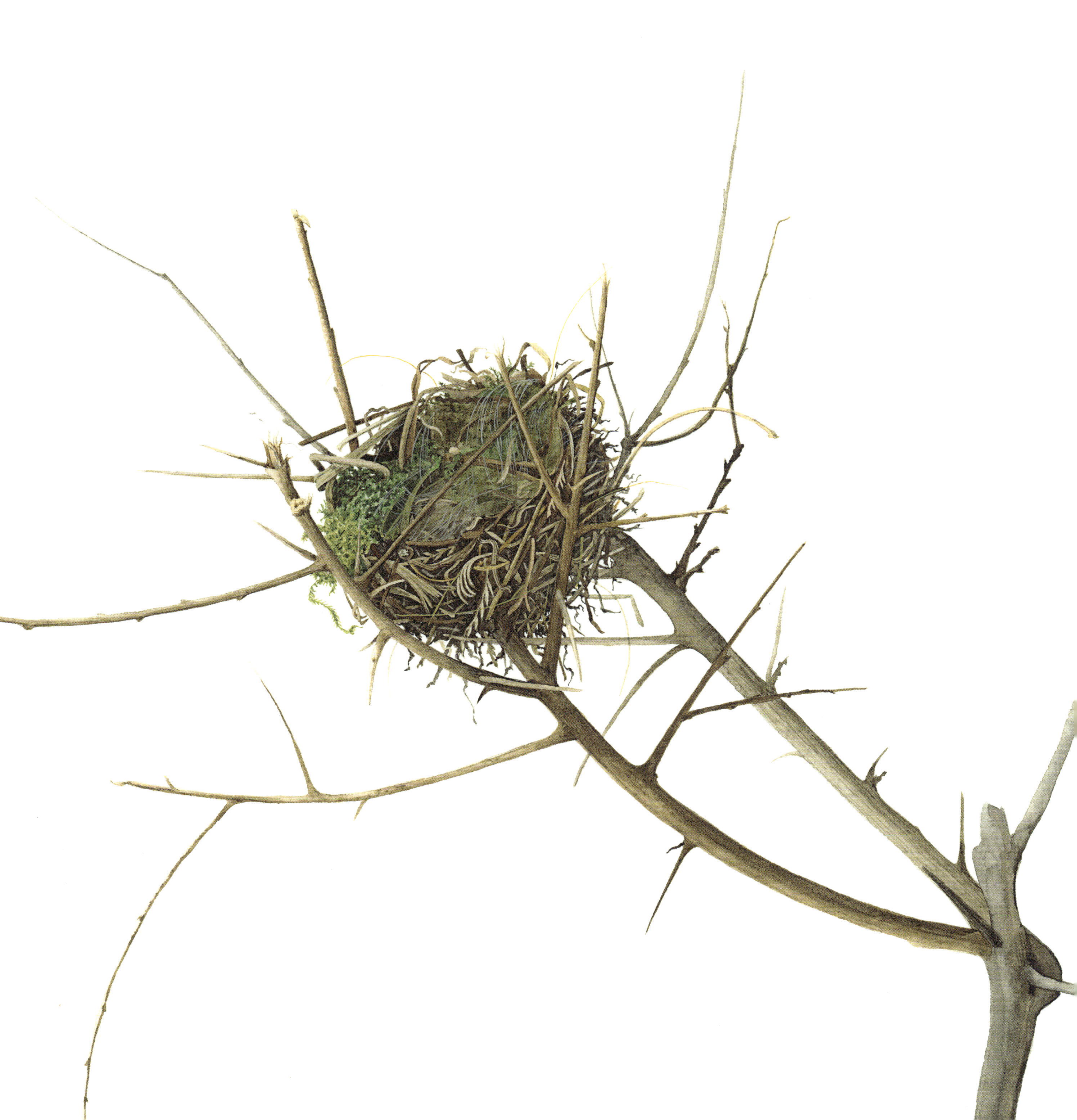

BLACKCAP

Sylvia atricapilla

Here is a chance to see a blackcap nest out of its position
within a bush. It is mainly built of grasses and cobwebs, with
a few tiny leaves and wisps of moss, and appears to be unlined,
suggesting that it is a cock nest.

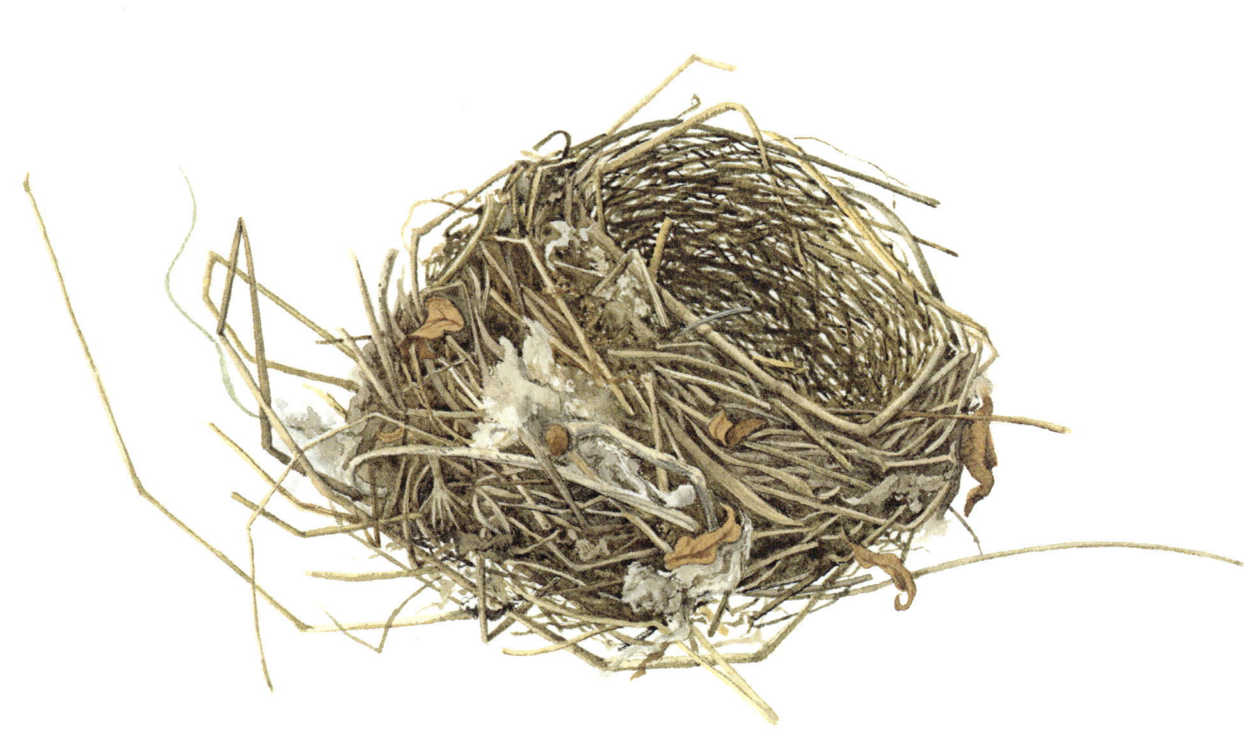

WHITETHROAT

Sylvia communis

Migrant	Arrives in April or May from as far away as Africa
Lifespan	About 5 years, although 8 years has been recorded
Diet	Insects in summer; berries in autumn before migration
Breeding season	May to July
Broods	1–2 clutches of 4–5 eggs
Position	Low down in brambles or nettles
Materials	Grass stems
Lining	Plant fluff, wool, fine grass

Sometimes called the nettle creeper, the whitethroat favours nettle beds and bramble thickets for its nesting sites. Like the wren and the blackcap, the male whitethroat builds several 'cock nests' before the female lines the one she selects. The nest is a deep cup of loosely woven grasses. Both parents share the incubation for eleven to thirteen days, and the feeding of the young for ten to twelve days. Whitethroats generally have two broods.

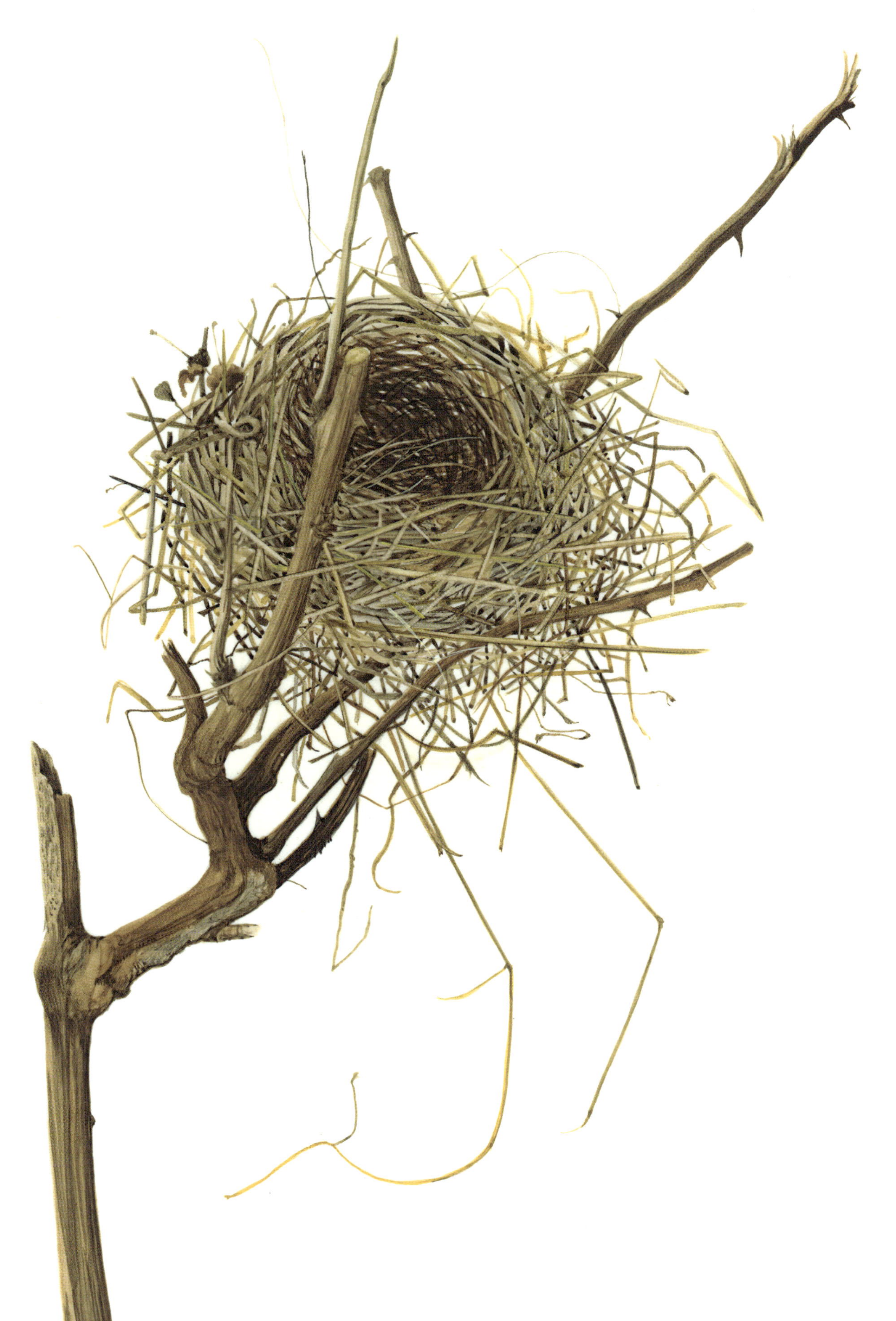

LESSER WHITETHROAT

Sylvia curruca

Migrant	Leaves Britain as early as mid-July
Lifespan	Up to 5 years, although 7 years has been recorded
Diet	Insects in summer, berries before migration
Breeding season	May to July
Broods	1–2 clutches of 4–6 eggs
Position	Low down in hawthorn, brambles and dense hedges
Materials	Grass, rootlets, cobwebs, stalks
Lining	Hair, moss

The lesser whitethroat is a migrant, returning to Britain from its African winter habitat in the spring. The male builds several incomplete 'cock nests', and once the female has chosen her preferred one, they finish it together. Both adults share the incubating of the eggs for ten to eleven days and also the care of the brood, which fledges after a further ten to eleven days, when only able to flutter. They can produce two broods before starting on their return trip around mid-July, when they head east, reaching Africa via the eastern Mediterranean.

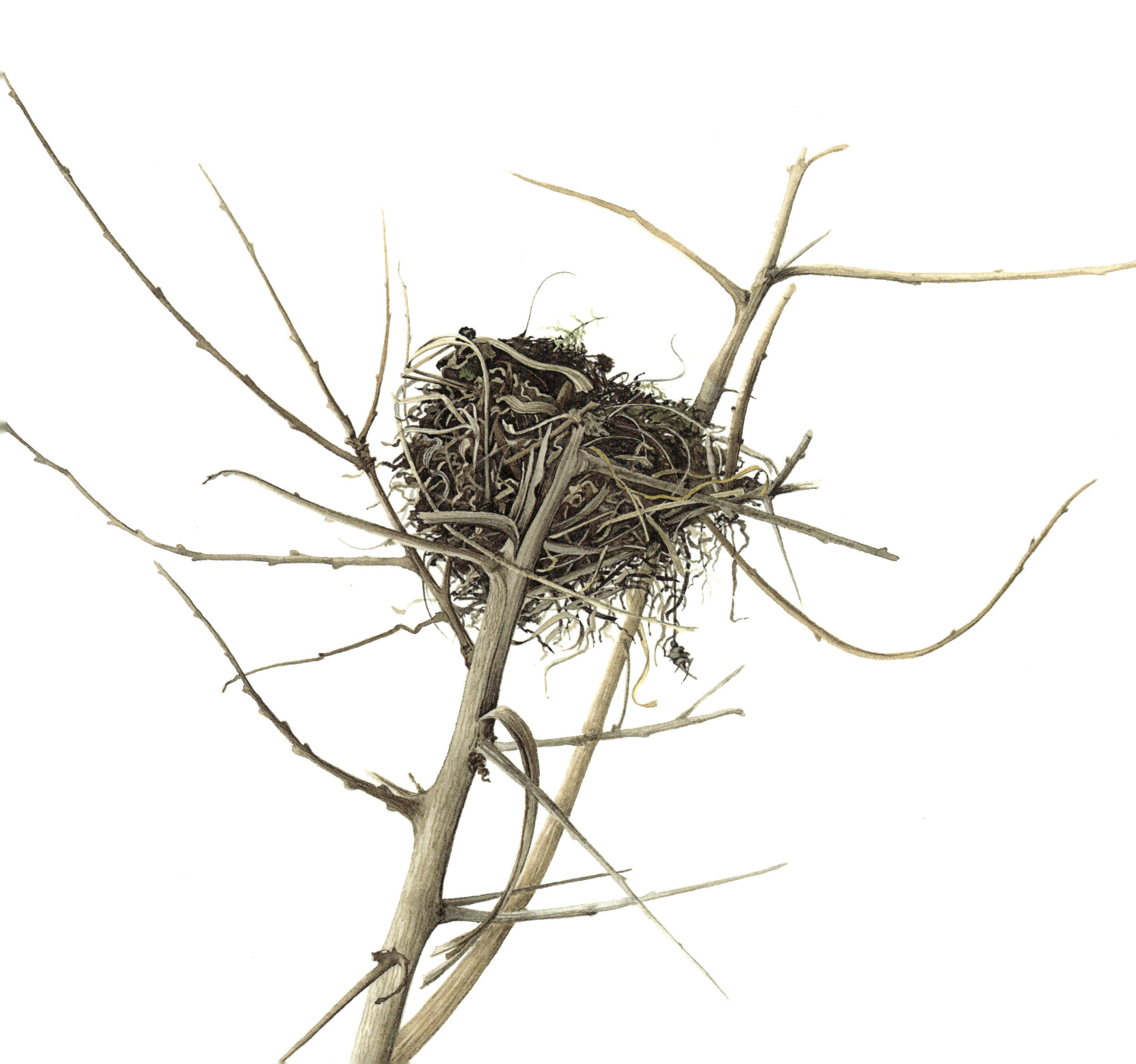

SPOTTED FLYCATCHER

Muscicapa striata

Migrant	A long-distance migrant, only in Britain for a few summer months
Lifespan	About 5 years, although 9 years has been recorded
Diet	Flying insects and butterflies caught on the wing; ground insects if necessary
Breeding season	May to July
Broods	1–2 clutches of 4–6 eggs
Position	On a sheltered ledge, among creepers on a wall or close to a tree trunk
Materials	Grasses, twigs, rootlets, lichen, spiders' webs, leaves
Lining	Hair, wool, fine grass, small feathers

The spotted flycatcher is a long-distance migrant that winters south of the equator – a remarkable distance to fly for a bird about the size of a sparrow. Both sexes build the nest, a deep cup of loosely woven twigs, spiders' webs, grasses, roots, lichen and leaves, before the female incubates the eggs for eleven to fifteen days. The parents share the feeding of the nestlings, continuing their care of the young for a further two or three weeks after they have fledged at twelve to fourteen days, although this may be delayed during bad weather.

Deon Warner found this beautiful nest in a stack of logs piled in a wood. There were two adults and three fledglings in the same patch of dead elm, which provided a good hunting ground, and for several days Deon watched the youngsters catching insects and returning to the same branches every time, to perch and wait for more insects.

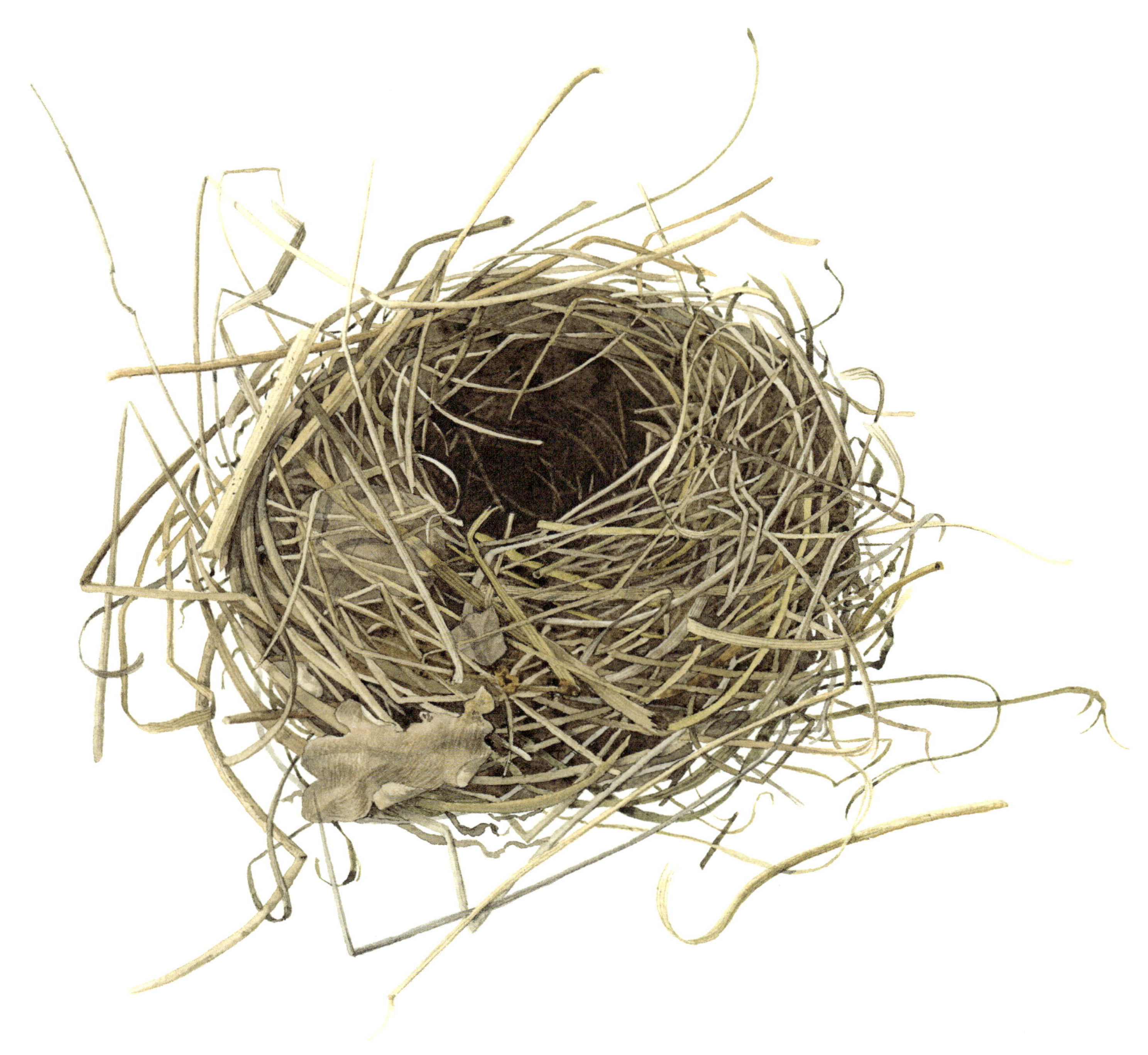

SPOTTED FLYCATCHER

Muscicapa striata

This nest was found in a garden. Its builder made use of moss, and lined it generously with thistledown. It is probably an older nest than the previous one, since much of the outside framework of grasses has gone and the leaves have started to rot.

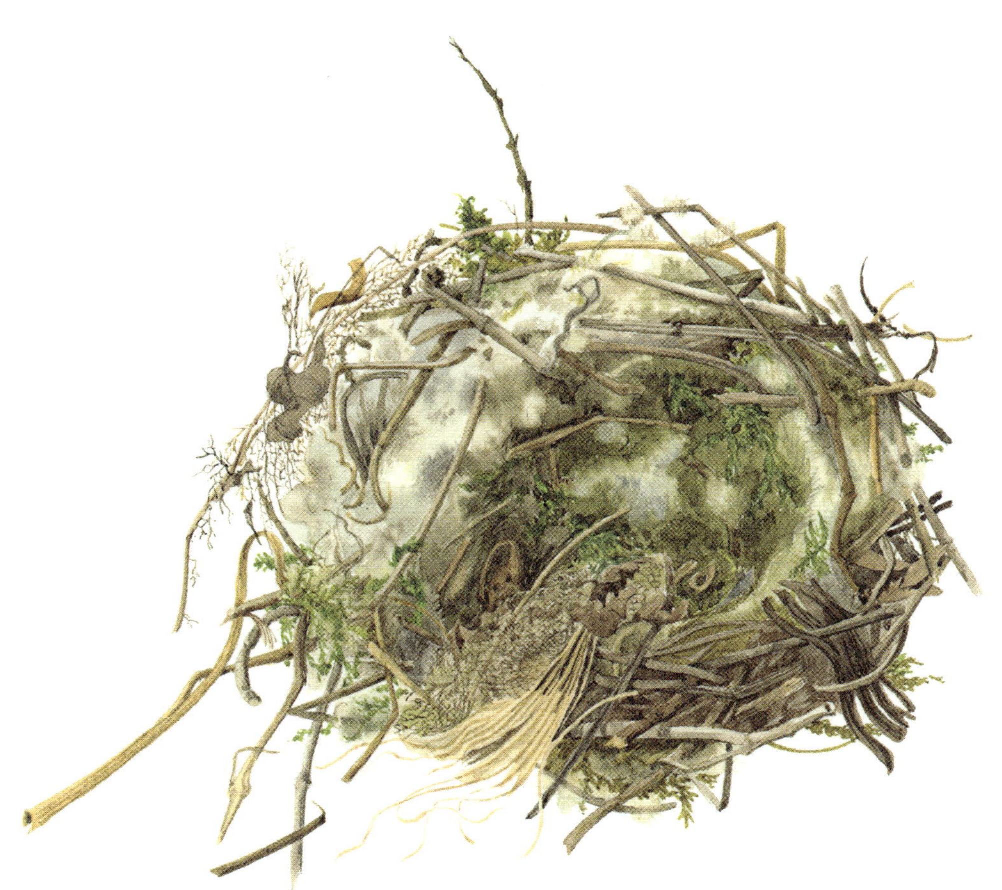

LONG-TAILED TIT

Aegithalos caudatus

Resident

Lifespan About 5 years, although 8 years has been recorded

Diet Insects, seeds

Breeding season April to June

Broods 1–2 clutches of 8–12 eggs

Position In thick shrubs or brambles, or in ivy on walls

Materials Moss, lichen, cobwebs, fine grass

Lining Small downy feathers

Built by both the male and female, the nest of the long-tailed tit is a miracle of carefully woven moss, lichen and grass, held firmly together with cobwebs to form a pouch with a small side entrance. The pouch is then lined with many downy feathers, positioned so that the quills point outwards to avoid damaging the eggs and the young; someone once counted about two thousand of them. You can see some of the tiny quills sticking out through the walls of this nest. It may look fragile, but its abundant use of cobweb makes this a strong, elastic home in which to rear a large brood of nestlings, and as they grow the nest can expand to accommodate them.

The hen incubates the eggs for twelve to fourteen days, and then the young are fed by both parents for a further fourteen to eighteen days. Once they have left the nest the parents continue to feed them for another ten to fourteen days. While painting this nest I put my finger through the hole and down into its depths. It felt like air, so softly was it lined.

The shape of the nest gives rise to the old name of bottle tit.

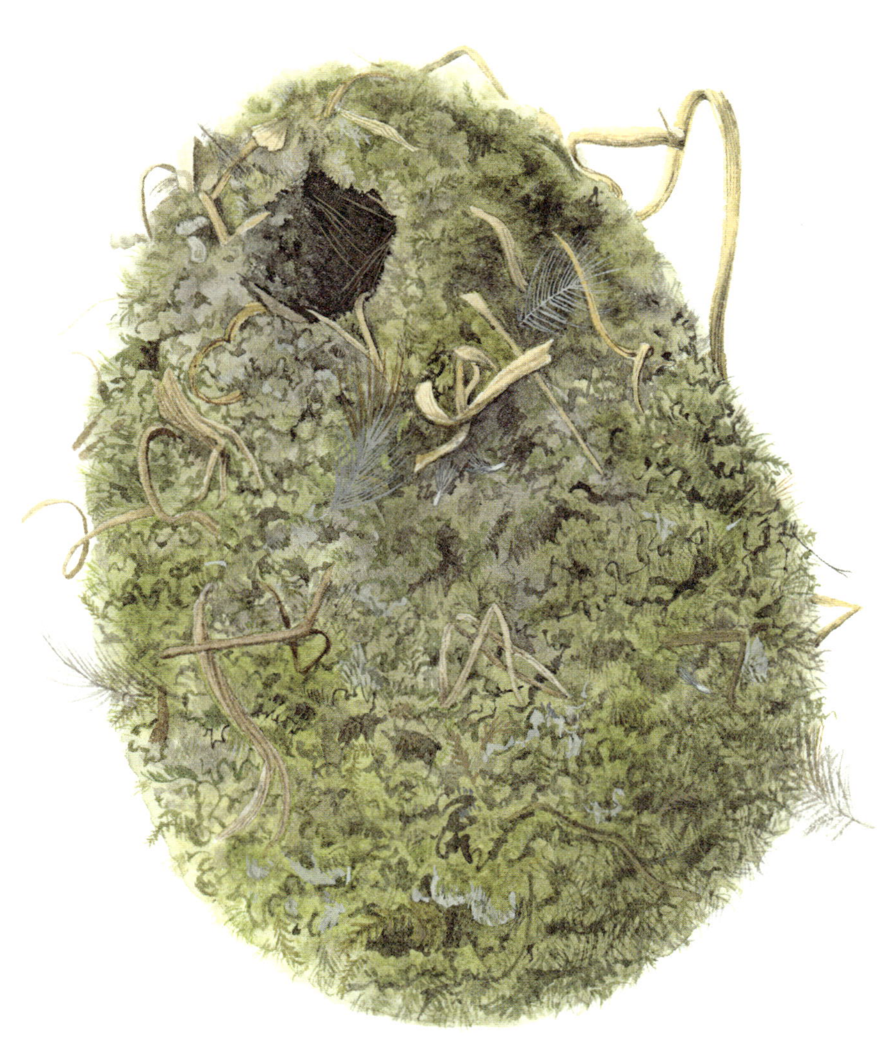

LONG-TAILED TIT

Aegithalos caudatus

The long-tailed tit nest on the previous page was an almost
perfect specimen, and this one probably looked much the same
when it was first built – but the moss has dried out and the top
has been lifted off by a raiding magpie. Still, it remains an
interesting nest that shows how it was anchored to its branch,
as well as the use of lichen as camouflage.

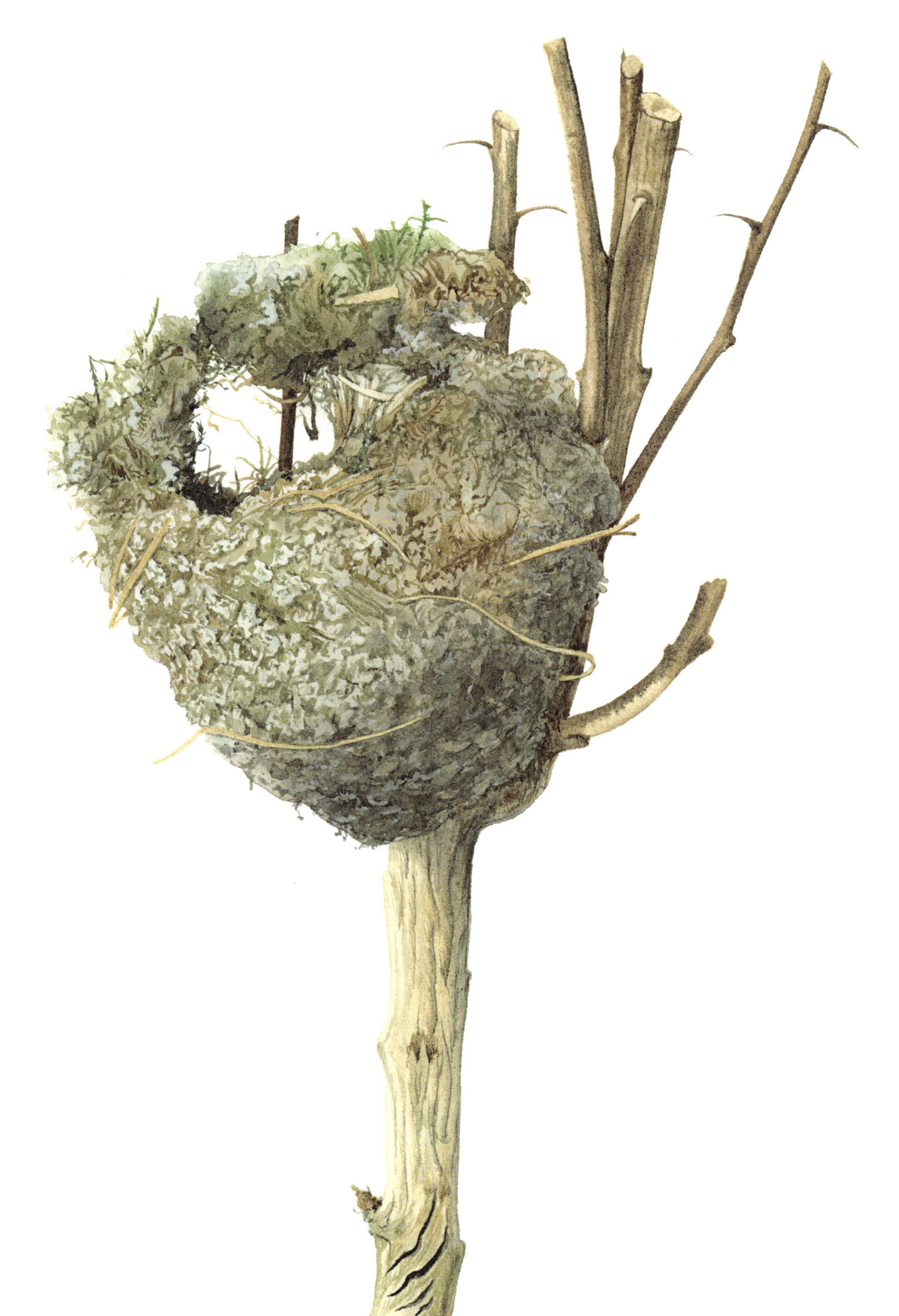

BLUE TIT
Cyanistes caeruleus

Resident	
Lifespan	2–3 years
Diet	Caterpillars, insects, seeds, nuts
Breeding season	Late March to June
Broods	1 clutch of up to 16 eggs
Position	In holes, crevices or nesting boxes
Materials	Moss, grasses, fine twigs, feathers, hair, spiders' webs
Lining	Moss, fine grass, feathers

The blue tit is a much loved little bird, able to perform clever acrobatic feats to reach its food. It generally nests in holes and crevices but readily adapts to nesting boxes. The nests are built almost entirely by the female, usually in April and May when the trees are coming into leaf and the resulting explosion of caterpillar numbers provides food for the chicks. Nests are built close to this food source because the nestlings can each eat a hundred of these tiny caterpillars in a day, so a family of ten will need a thousand – a vast number for the parents to find. The nest is made of grass, moss and twigs, lined with wool, hair and feathers, and takes one to two weeks to build. The blue tit has one of the largest clutches of all birds, with eight to twelve eggs, and up to sixteen. The female incubates the eggs for twelve to sixteen days, and both parents feed the young for fifteen to twenty-three days in the nest. Second broods are rare.

It has been estimated that during the winter small birds such as blue tits and goldcrests have to consume as much as thirty per cent of their body weight in order to maintain their fat reserves and survive the long, cold nights. Because there is safety in numbers they form flocks with other tits and chaffinches in order to raid fields for seeds during daylight hours, and roost together at night.

I found this nest in the eaves of a low roof, and it includes a wisp of roof insulation. It had been abandoned and contained several broken eggs, having been raided by a house sparrow. This means the nest has not been flattened by the exertions of a large family, and has retained its original shape.

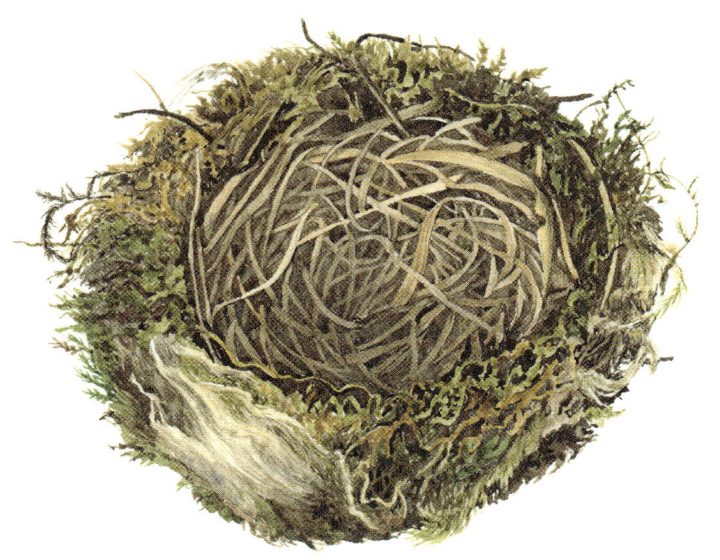

BLUE TIT

Cyanistes caeruleus

The square shape of this specimen shows that it was built in
a nesting box and has been flattened by the large family it
housed. It was fixed on to the side of a barn on the Isle of Arran
and contains stiff deer hair, a material readily found in the area.
The barn was being converted into a kitchen and the parents
flew endlessly backwards and forwards to feed their young,
bravely dodging builders and bulldozers. Care was taken
to disturb them as little as possible, but so devoted were they
to their task that nothing distracted them.

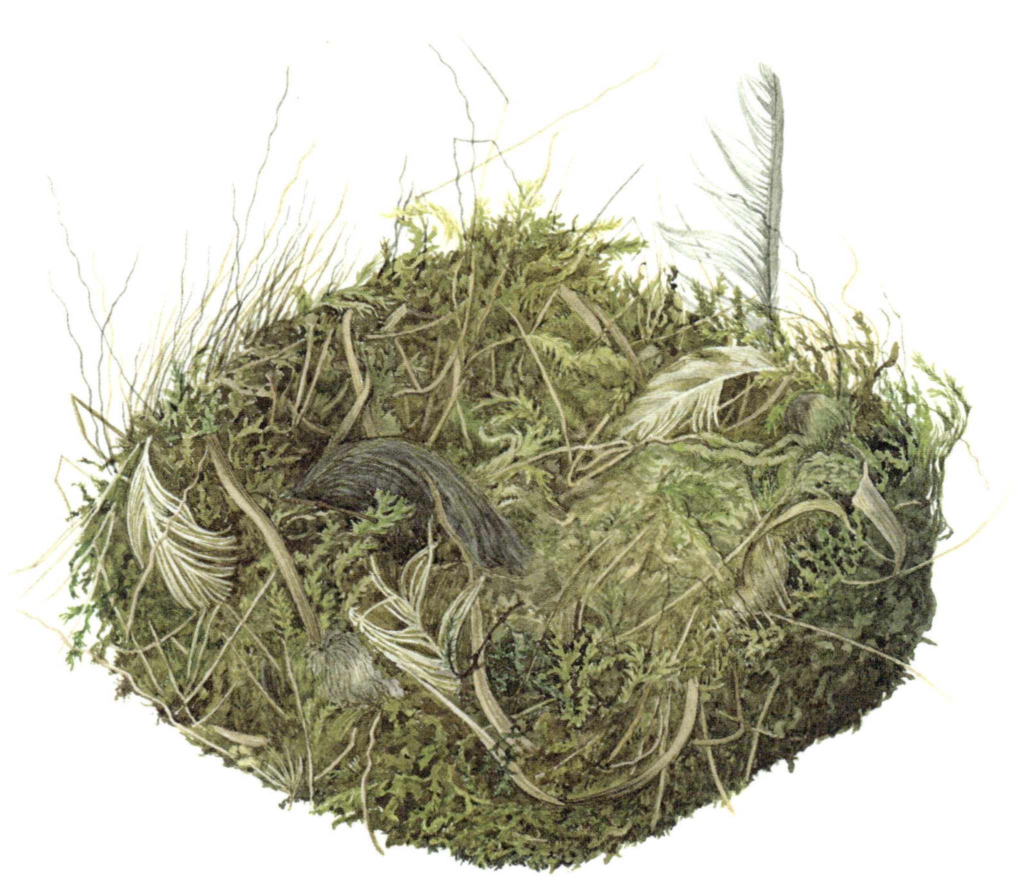

GREAT TIT

Parus major

Resident

Lifespan	2–3 years
Diet	Mainly insects and caterpillars in summer, seeds and nuts in winter
Breeding season	Late March to June
Broods	1–2 clutches of 5–12 eggs
Position	In crevices in walls, holes in trees or banks, or even letterboxes
Materials	Moss, grass, wool, hair, roots, lichen, plant down, spiders' webs
Lining	Plant down, hair, wool

The great tit appears throughout Britain, but is most abundant in the central and southern areas of the country. It favours deciduous woodland but will visit more open spaces to collect food.

The female builds the nest in a cavity in a tree, bank or building, or will use a well-screened nesting box. She makes a neat ring of moss, lining it with fur, hair or feathers before laying a clutch of five to twelve eggs – sometimes even as many as fifteen – and then incubating them alone for thirteen to fourteen days. Both parents share the feeding of the young for about three weeks; at this point the fledglings leave the nest, but continue to be fed for a few more days. Great tits may produce two broods.

This nest was found by a friend, an expert on birds, in her garden. Suspecting that they might be useful to nest builders, she had put the combings from her long-haired cat out on her bird table, and they turned up in the lining, along with some bits of coloured wool. The nest contained seven eggs, but the hen bird was taken by a sparrowhawk.

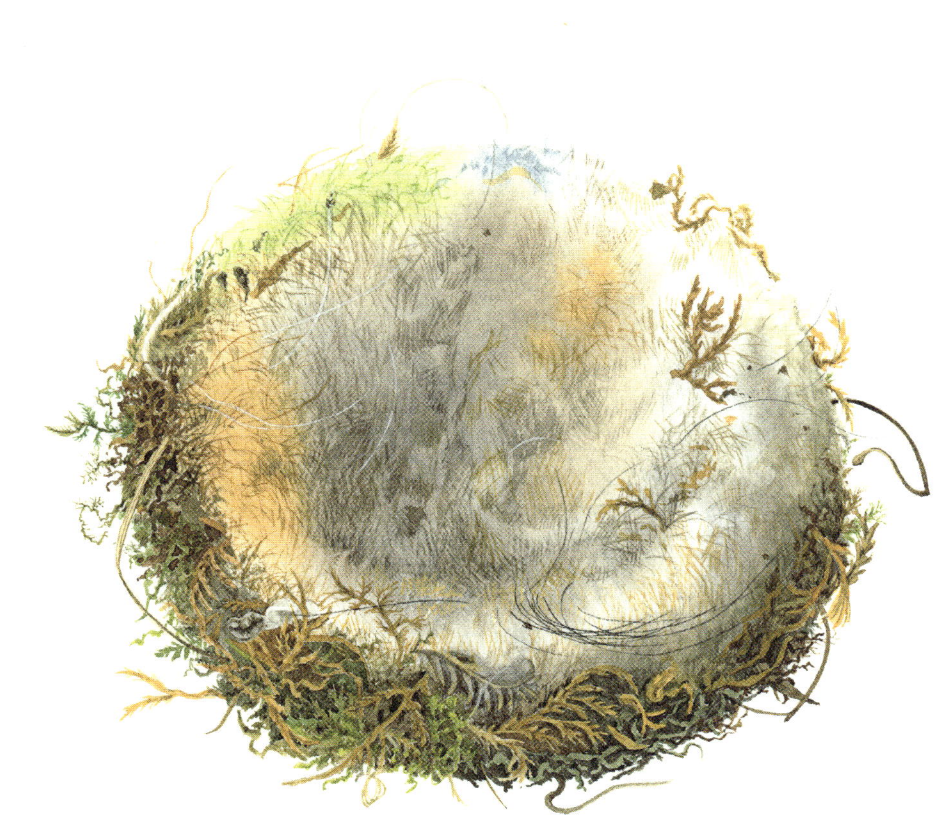

HOUSE SPARROW

Passer domesticus

<table>
<tr><td>*Resident*</td><td></td></tr>
<tr><td>*Lifespan*</td><td>About 3 years, although 12 years has been recorded</td></tr>
<tr><td>*Diet*</td><td>Adults feed on almost anything, including seeds, invertebrates, scavenged household scraps; nestlings on aphids and caterpillars</td></tr>
<tr><td>*Breeding season*</td><td>April to July</td></tr>
<tr><td>*Broods*</td><td>3 clutches of about 5 eggs, occasionally as many as 8 eggs</td></tr>
<tr><td>*Position*</td><td>Usually in the eaves of houses and barns, or in ivy on walls</td></tr>
<tr><td>*Materials*</td><td>Grasses, feathers</td></tr>
<tr><td>*Lining*</td><td>Feathers</td></tr>
</table>

The house sparrow is found on every continent except Antarctica, and seems unconcerned by the presence of humans, often living in cities and nesting in the eaves of houses.

House sparrows mate for life and both adults build the nest, an untidy base of grasses with a mass of feathers forming the cup. These nests are generally domed, with a side entrance, but if the chosen site itself provides sufficient roofing, the dome is reduced to not much more than a nod towards architectural convention. The nest here was in a nesting box – hence the minimal roof. It has been built and lined with a liberal helping of pigeon feathers, as well as bits of tissue and a piece of dark green chiffon tucked in between the feathers and grasses.

The hen lays about five eggs. Both adults share the incubation of eleven to fourteen days, although the female does most of it. Feeding of the nestlings is also shared. The young fledge at between fourteen and sixteen days, but continue to be fed for a further two or three weeks.

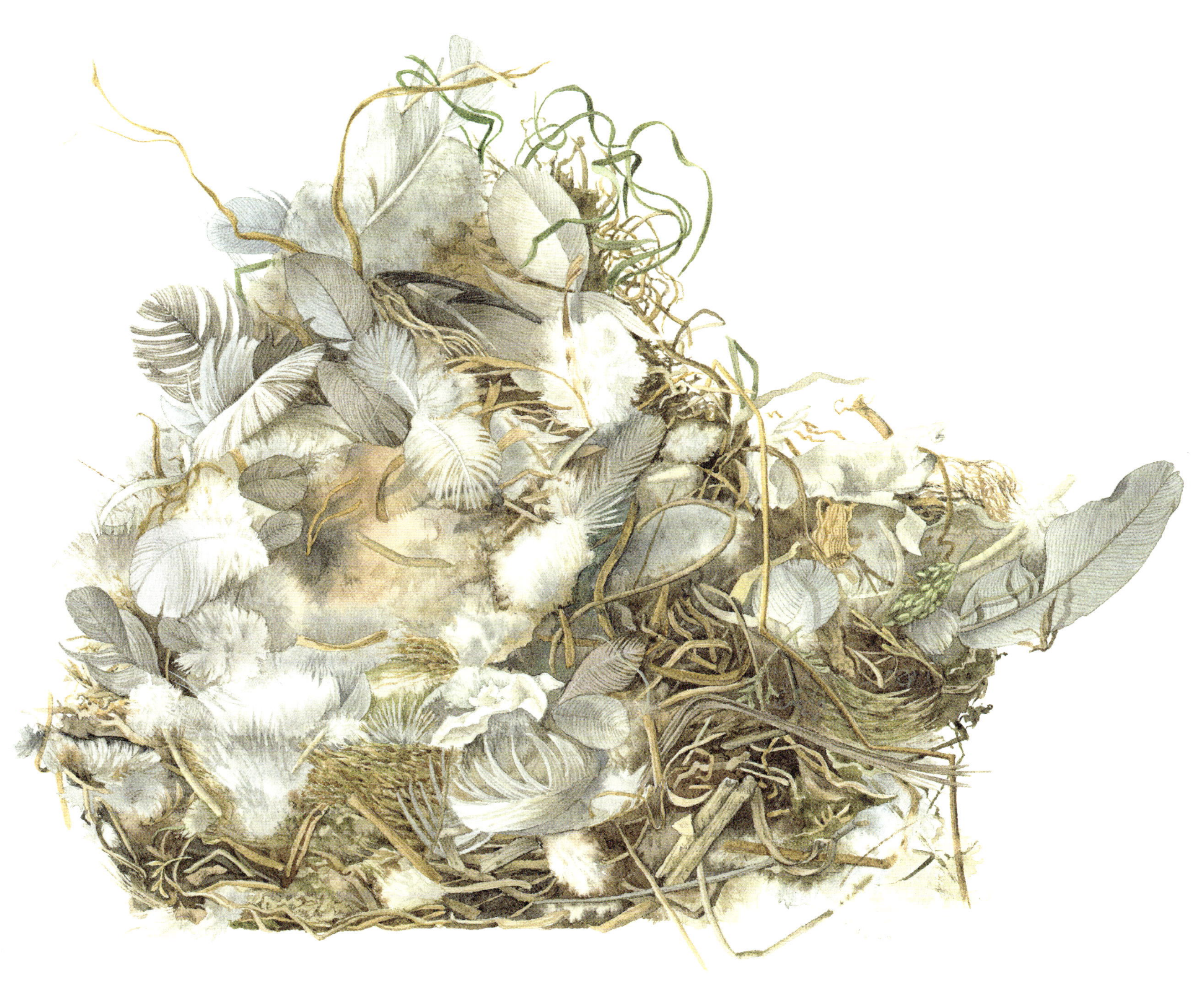

HOUSE SPARROW

Passer domesticus

I love this nest. It's completely bonkers, and appears to have
been built by house sparrows with delusions of grandeur.
It was found in the gable end of our house – only about six feet
above my head as I sit at my desk – and once all activity had
ceased I simply went up into the attic to collect it. It had been
built on a small window ledge reached from the outside
through a terracotta pipe built into the wall for ventilation.
The pipe had some crumpled wire netting stuffed into it to
deter birds, but these house sparrows were clearly made of
sterner stuff, and were not going to let that stop them. The
'sweeping drive' up to the nest includes some very large pigeon
feathers; it must have taken much determination to grapple
them through the wire netting and into place.

The whole construction was 33cm in length, so extended
beyond the size of this page. The birds had filled the space
on the ledge before forming the nest itself – the same small,
cosy shelter as any other house sparrow nest.

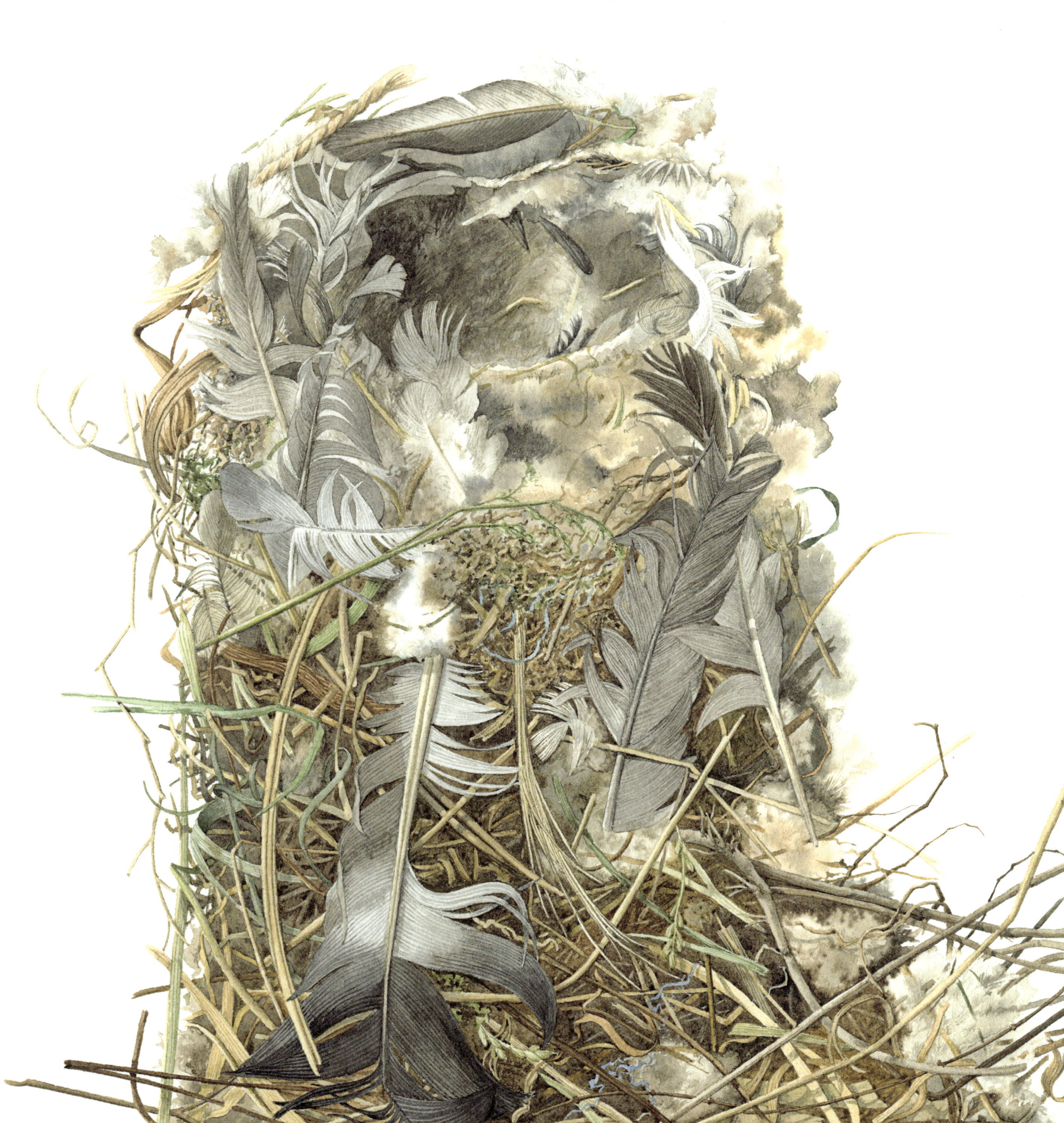

LINNET
Linaria cannabina

Resident	
Lifespan	2–3 years
Diet	Seeds, insects
Breeding season	April to June
Broods	2–3 clutches of 4–6 eggs
Position	Close to the ground in dense bushes and hedges
Materials	Rootlets, grass, lichen, small twigs
Lining	Plant down, hair, wool

The linnet nests on rough wasteland, farmland and in rural gardens, building its nest in low bushes and shrubs like gorse or bramble. The female builds the nest and incubates her eggs for ten to fourteen days. Both parents feed the young for ten to twelve days, until they fledge, and then for a further fortnight after they have left the nest. Unusually, they feed their young on seeds. Multiple pairs of linnets may nest in close association in adjacent bushes.

This nest is an example of a second nest built within the first one, probably for a second brood. Many species of bird do this, recycling the materials of the earlier nest to build the new one.

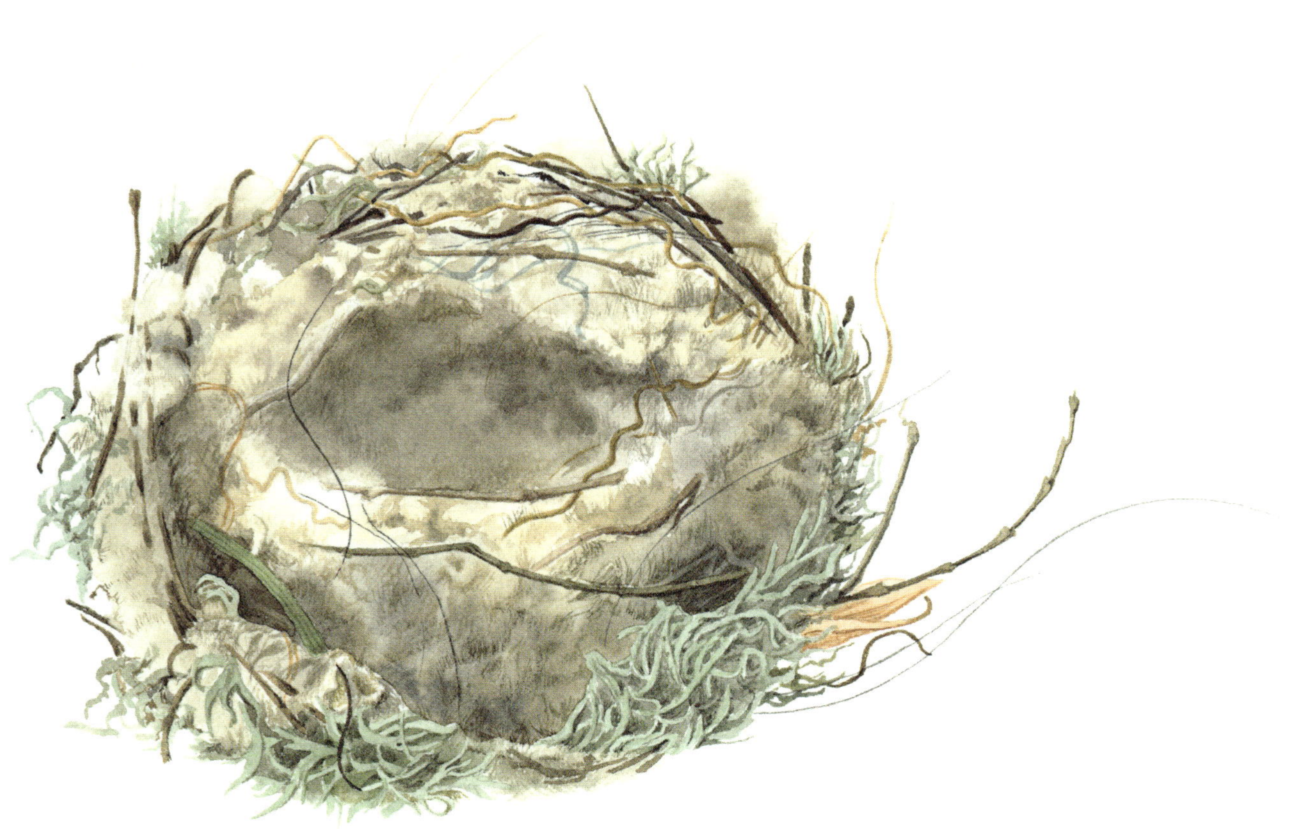

GOLDFINCH
Carduelis carduelis

Partial migrant	Some birds winter as far south as Spain
Lifespan	2–3 years
Diet	Insects, seeds
Breeding season	May to July
Broods	2–3 clutches of 4–6 eggs
Position	High up in trees, on ends of branches
Materials	Moss, small twigs, rootlets, lichen, cobwebs
Lining	Hair, wool, thistledown, dandelion petals, sometimes feathers

The goldfinch is one of our more brightly coloured birds and is seen throughout Britain, particularly where seeds are to be found – in open land, gardens and roadside verges.

The nest – a tidy little cup of roots, moss and lichen lined with thistledown, hair and feathers – is built by the female. (This example also contains a few strands of shredded orange baler twine.) Although it looks precarious in its position towards the end of a swaying branch in a small tree or shrub, it is firmly attached with spiders' web. It takes about a week to build. These sociable birds sometimes breed in colonies. The female incubates the eggs for eleven to thirteen days and both parents feed the young for twelve to sixteen days, caring for the fledglings for another week after they leave the nest. There are usually two or three broods.

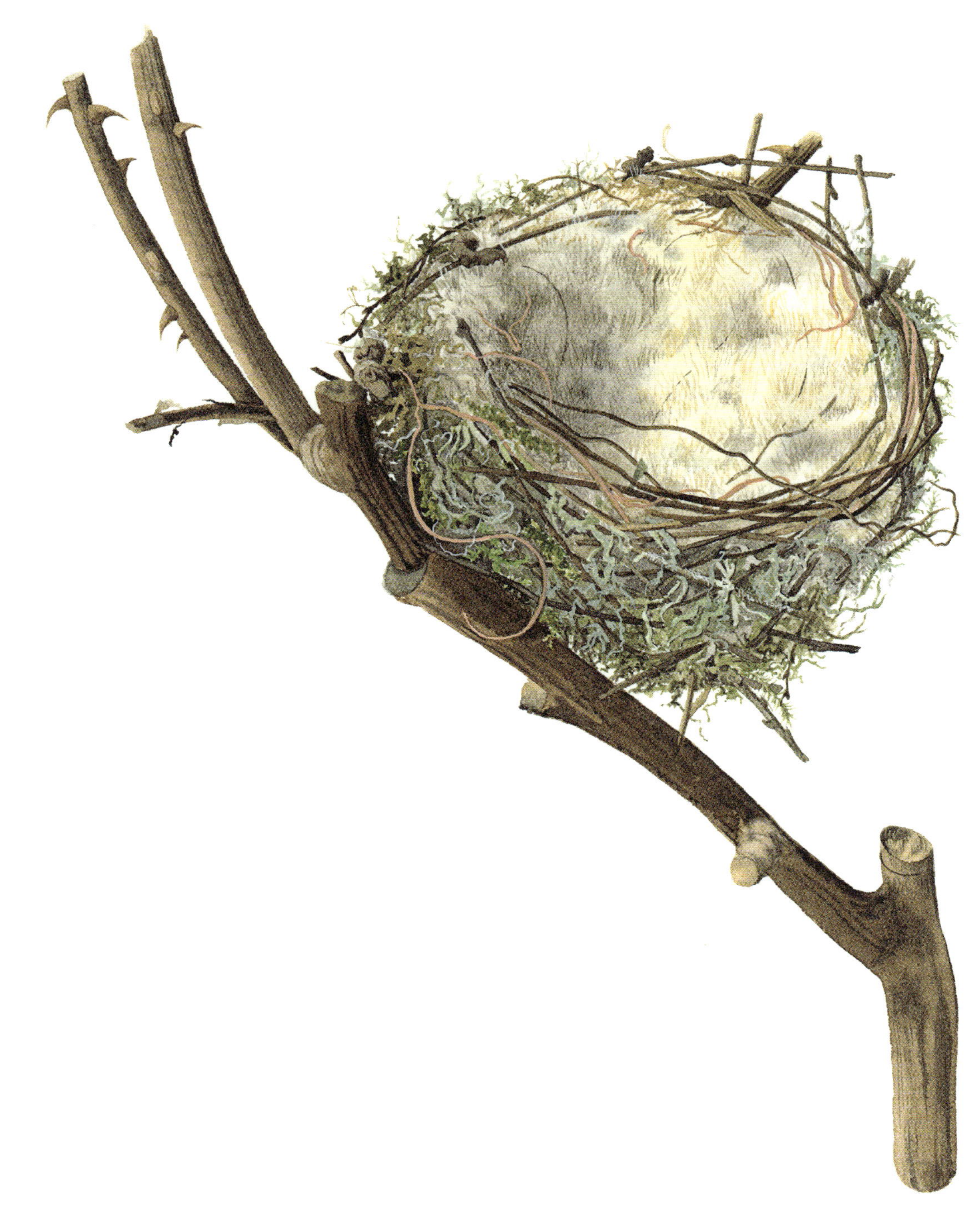

GOLDFINCH
Carduelis carduelis

A friend found this nest lying on the verge of the lane where I live. We admired its liberal use of blue baler twine, and Deon Warner identified it as the work of the colourful little goldfinch. Once again, this is an example of the instinctive nest-building technique of a species adapted to make use of locally found materials.

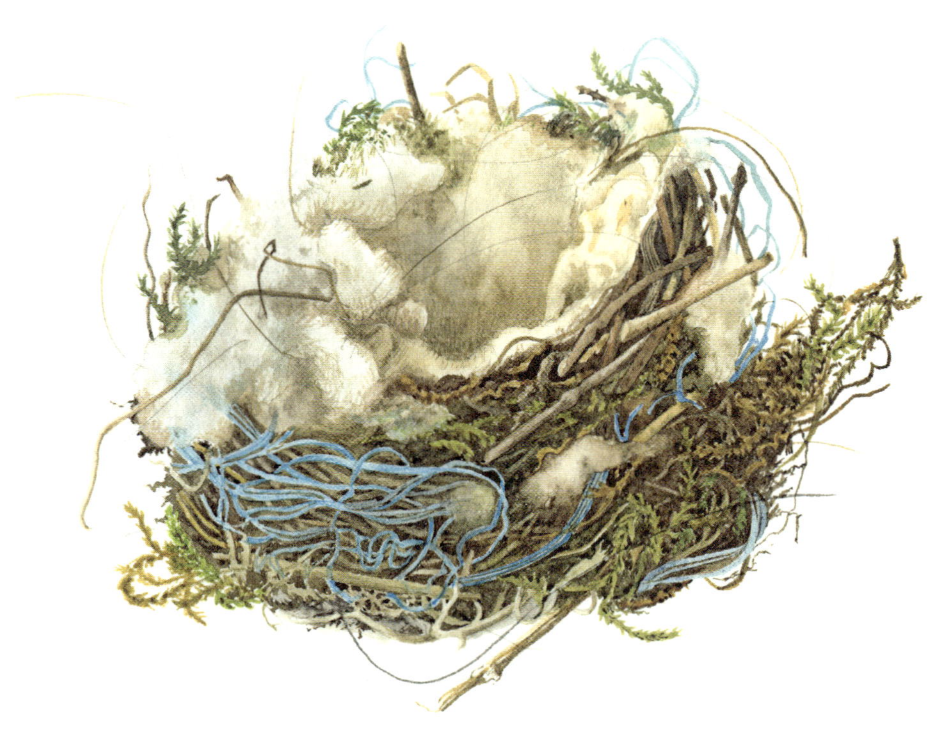

GOLDFINCH
Carduelis carduelis

This nest was found in a bay tree in south-east London. It has all the usual hallmarks of a goldfinch nest, but as I painted it I realized that much of the construction seemed to be from materials used for upholstery – kapok, polyester wadding and coir or jute fibres. Perhaps this resourceful little bird found an old chair in a skip and made good use of it.

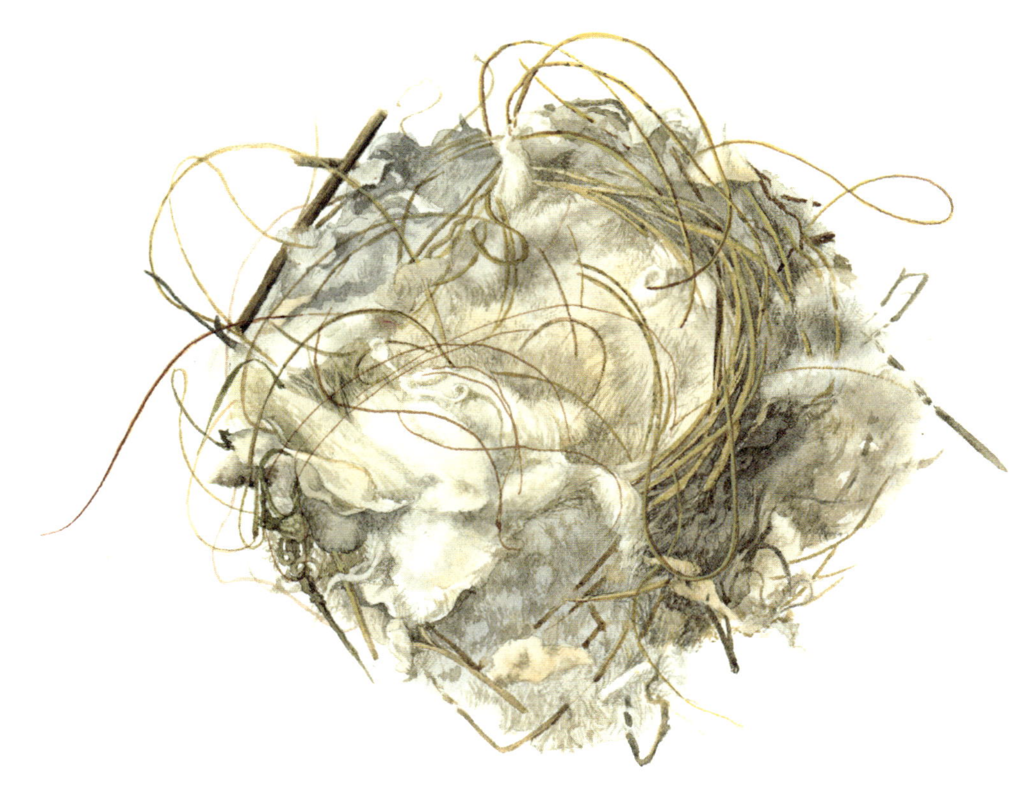

GOLDFINCH

Carduelis carduelis

Unlike the other goldfinch nests I have painted, this one is
lined with feathers. It was found on the ground after a storm.
It is such a pretty nest and so beautifully constructed that its
abrupt end is a shame, but it has given great pleasure to those
who can now admire it.

It was found by a small great-niece of mine, who lives in
my father's old house. He would be delighted to know that
his great-granddaughter was pottering around in his garden
finding nests.

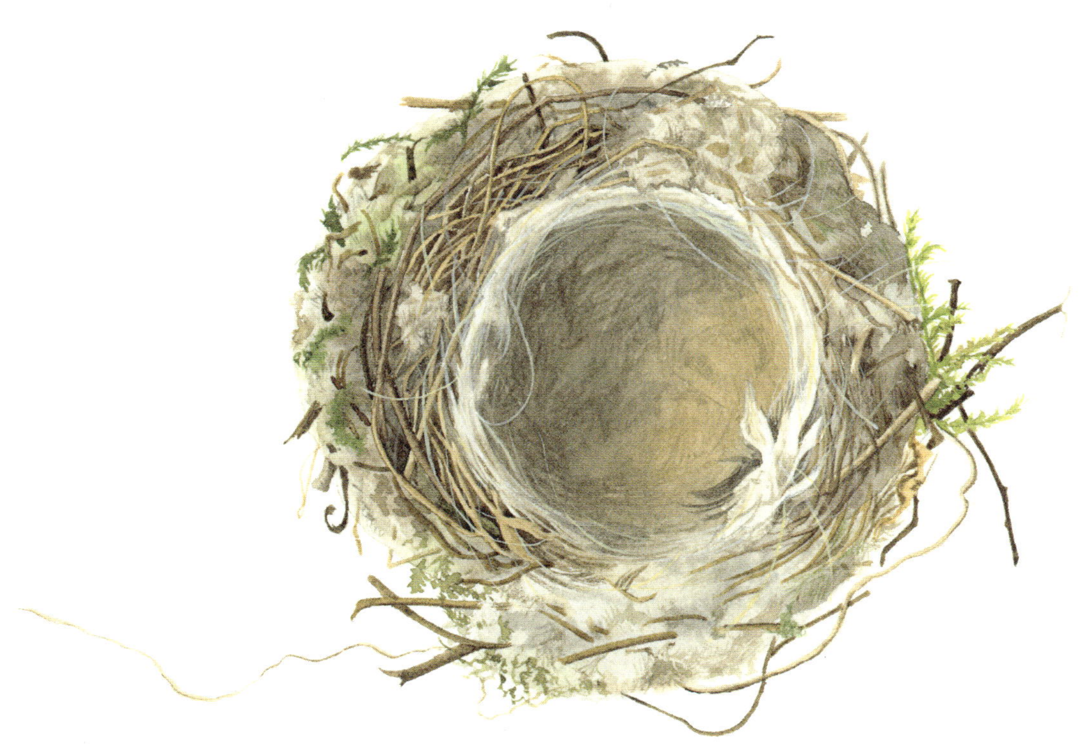

GOLDFINCH
Carduelis carduelis

Here is an example of one nest built on top of another. At first
Deon Warner and I simply wondered at its unusual shape,
with a heightened construction but a standard depth of cup.
But once I examined it closely I could see that there was
a slight layer of lining halfway down, and that the bottom half
appeared to be older and greyer than the top half, which led me
to conclude that this is a 'double decker', with the second nest
built on top of the first.

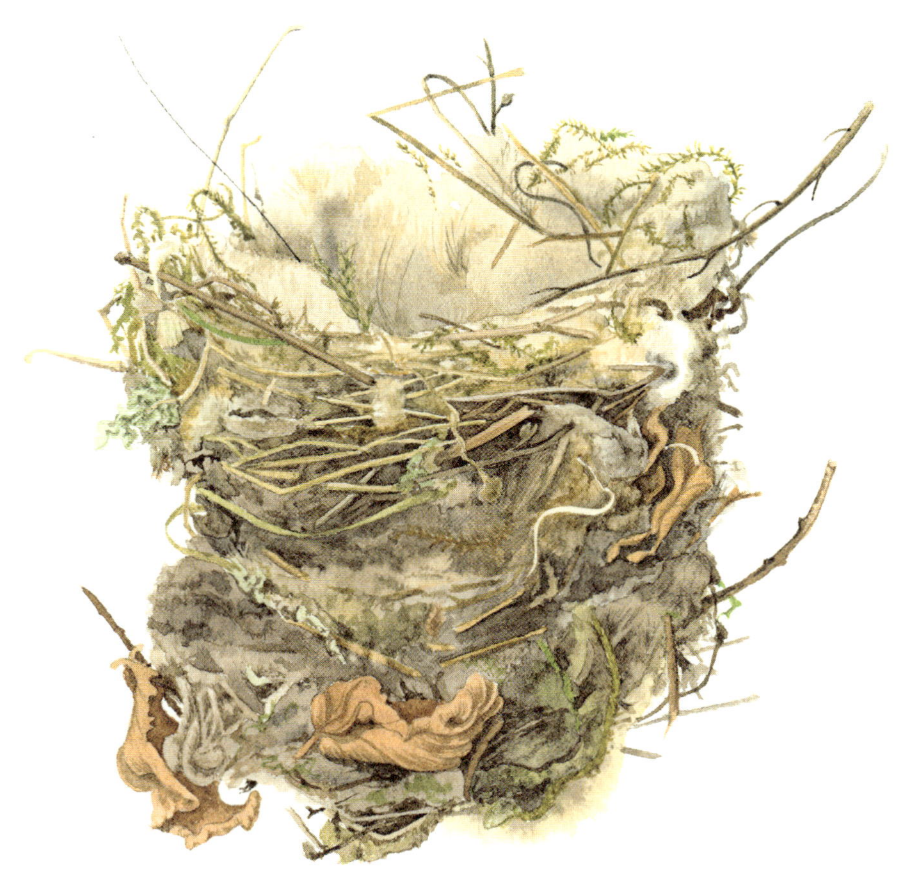

GOLDFINCH

Carduelis carduelis

Here is a particularly pretty goldfinch nest made with
lichen-covered twigs and lined with wool. It was found by
a friend who lives beside the River Parrett, on a bank where
she has noticed much lichen growing.

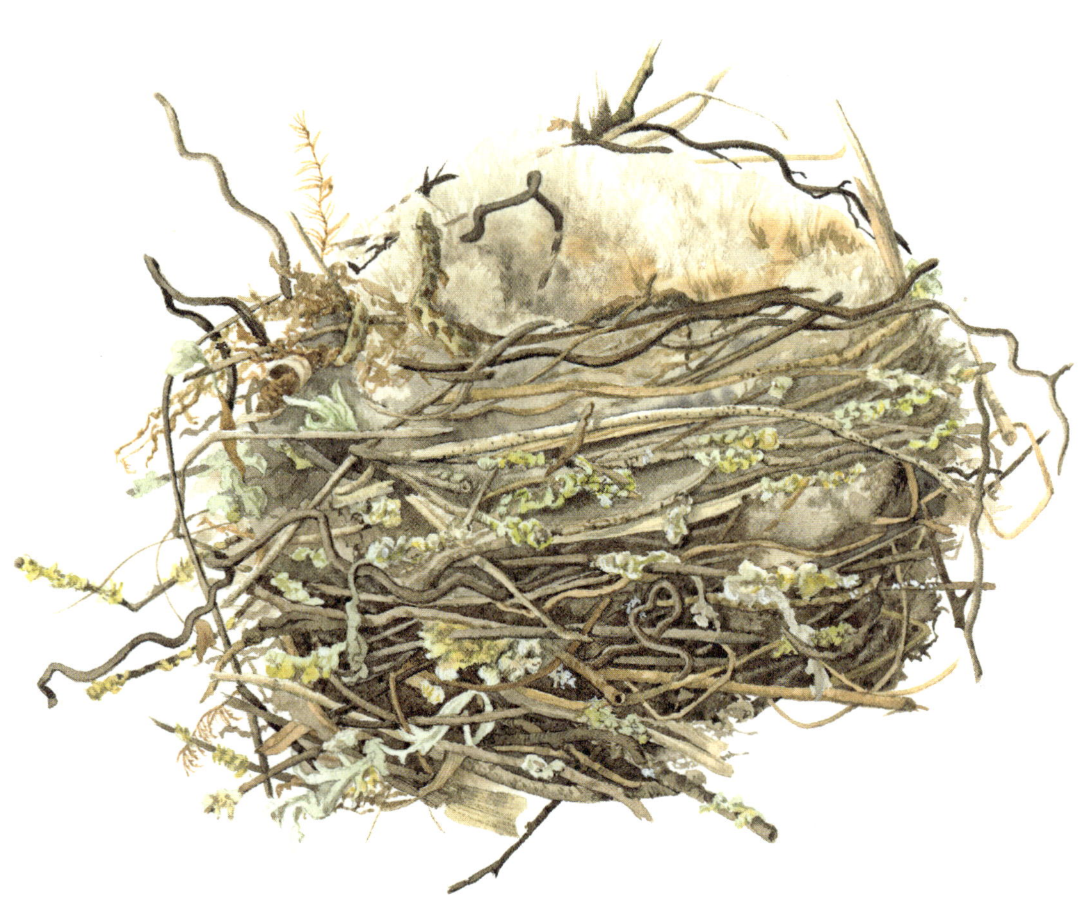

GREENFINCH

Chloris chloris

Partial migrant	Some northern British birds migrate to southern Britain or Europe
Lifespan	About 5 years, although 12 years has been recorded
Diet	Seeds, grains
Breeding season	April to July
Broods	2–3 clutches of 4–6 eggs
Position	In woods, gardens and farmland with tall hedges
Materials	Fine twigs, rootlets, hair, grass, moss
Lining	Hair, grass, roots, plant down, feathers

The greenfinch is a partial migrant that winters further south than its breeding area. The female builds the nest of fine twigs and rootlets and much horsehair (or, occasionally, nylon fishing line) in a dense shrub or small tree. Once she has incubated the eggs for twelve to fourteen days the male joins her in feeding the nestlings until they fledge at thirteen to sixteen days. He continues this task if she starts another nest and brood. They will produce two or three broods in a season.

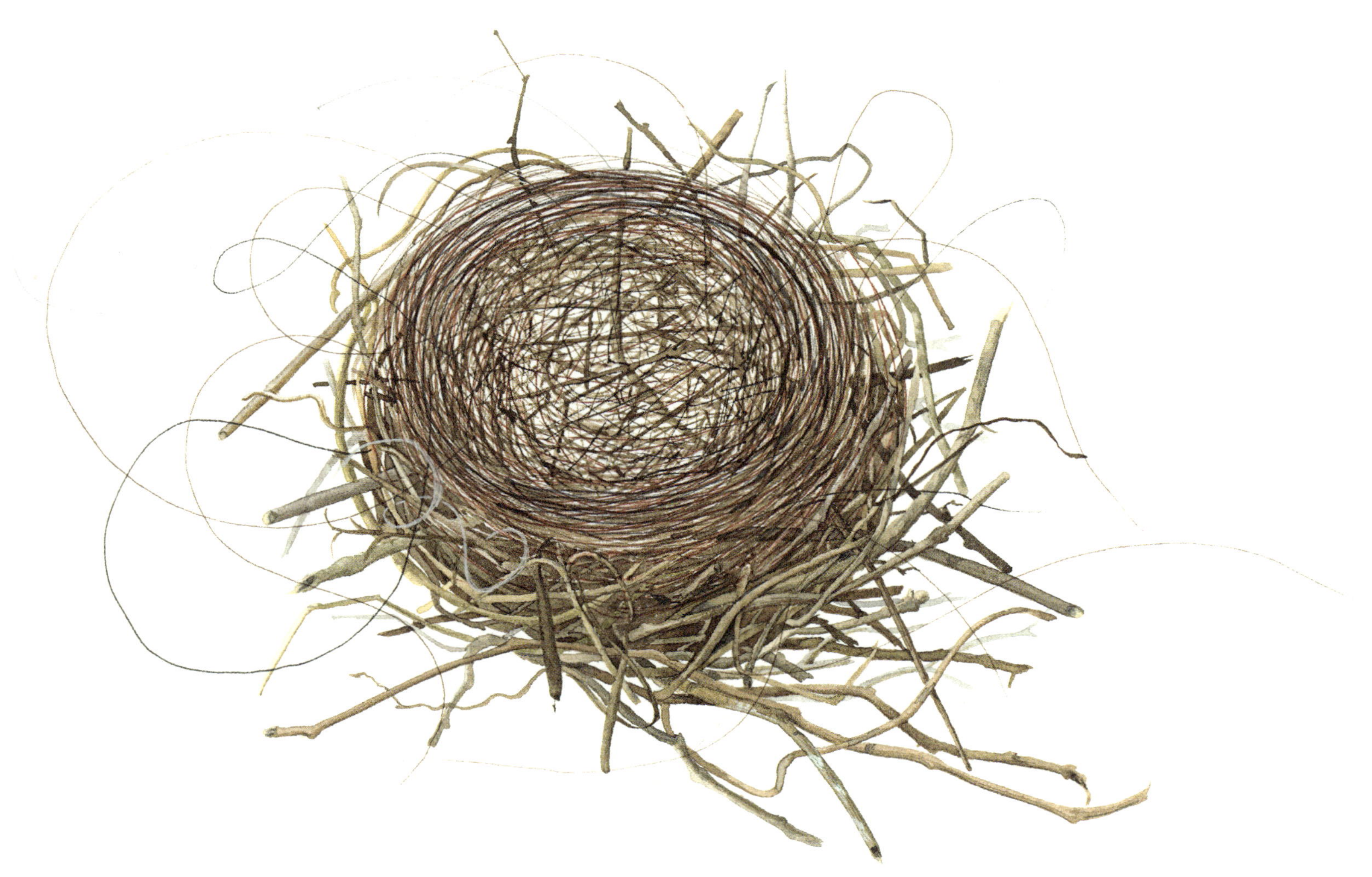

GREENFINCH

Chloris chloris

This greenfinch nest was found in a bay tree being pruned
by friends who are gardeners. It has been lined with feathers,
hair and plant down rather than just the hair used in the nest
shown on the previous page. When Becky found it the lining
had been pulled out and was caught beside the nest. Inside
the lining were several field maple seeds, some half eaten.
I showed it to Deon Warner, who concluded that the nest was
probably raided by a wood mouse which ate the eggs, then used
it as a larder. I tucked the lining back into place for this painting
in order to show the nest as it would have been built.

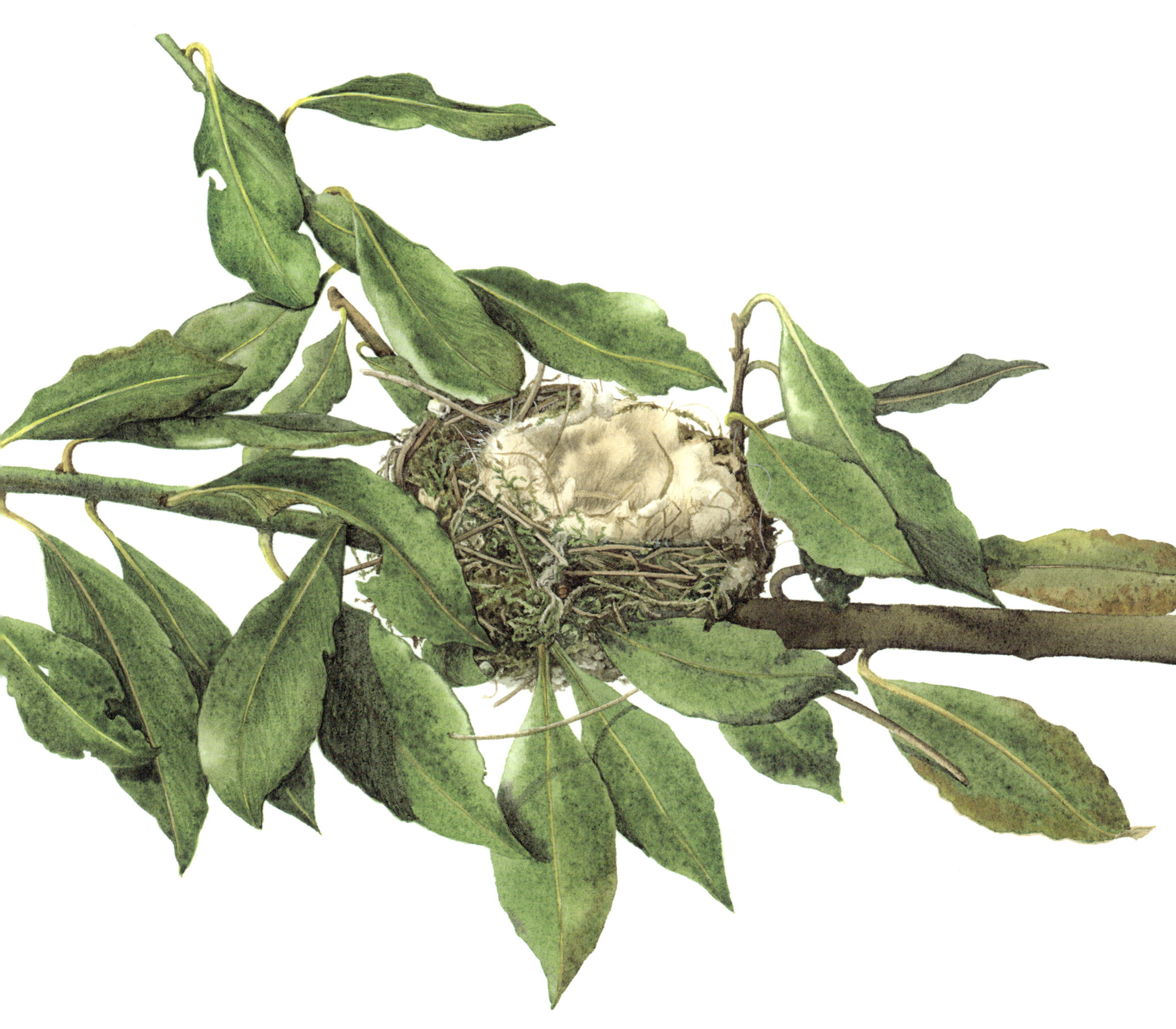

GREENFINCH

Chloris chloris

This greenfinch nest shows the use of much horsehair
as lining, as in the first nest, but its bowl has been flattened
and widened slightly by use. The whole structure was well
camouflaged with moss.

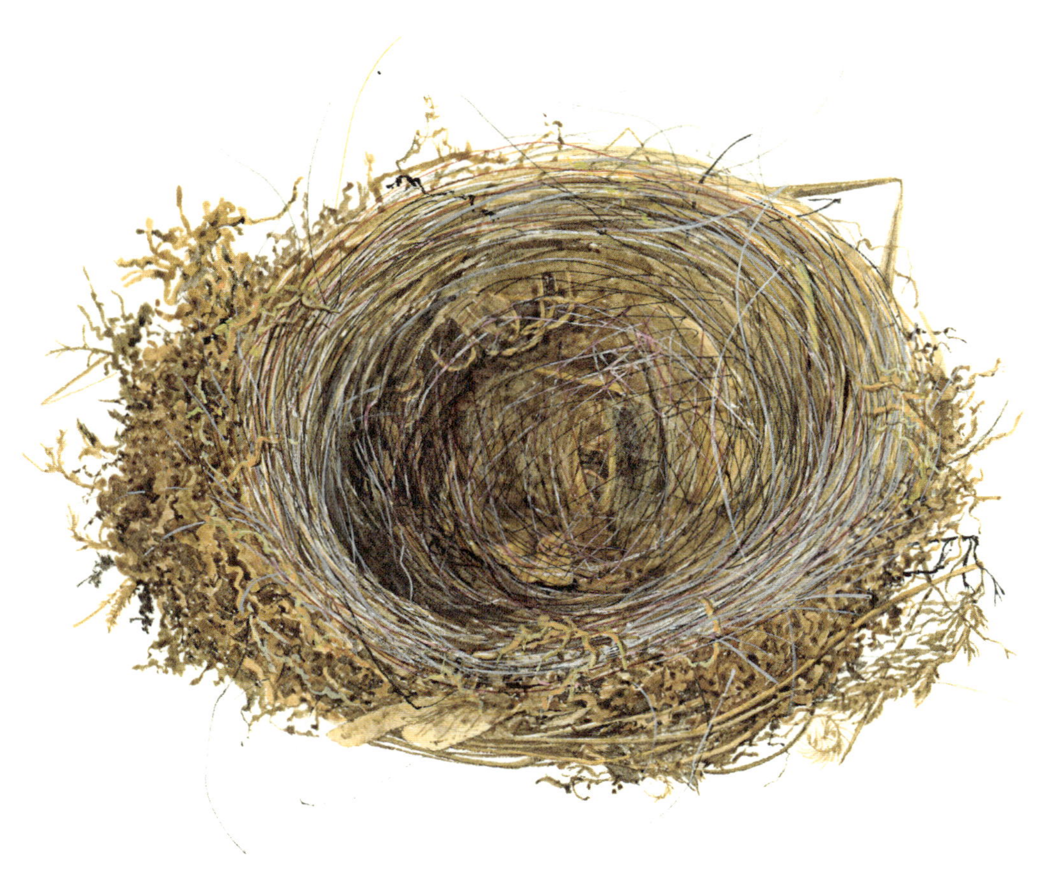

CHAFFINCH

Fringilla coelebs

Resident	
Lifespan	2–5 years
Diet	Insects, seeds
Breeding season	April to June
Broods	1–2 clutches of 4–5 eggs, but varies between 2 and 8
Position	In dense hedges or evergreens, or in forks of moss-clad trees
Materials	Moss, wool, lichen, grass, cobwebs
Lining	Feathers, hair

Chaffinches are widespread throughout Britain, nesting wherever trees or bushes exist to provide cover for their beautiful nests. These are wonderfully neat creations of mainly moss and lichen, held together with cobwebs and lined with feathers and hair. The addition of lichen is partly decorative and partly for camouflage, so varies according to the site of the nest. The female takes one to two weeks to build the nest, and incubates her eggs for eleven to fourteen days, starting the incubation from the second to last egg. The male then assists with the feeding of the young, who fledge at twelve to fifteen days. They rear one or two broods in a season.

This is the nest I found, sodden and unrecognizable, that opened my eyes to the whole wonder of avian architecture and started the adventure that absorbed me for the next five years.

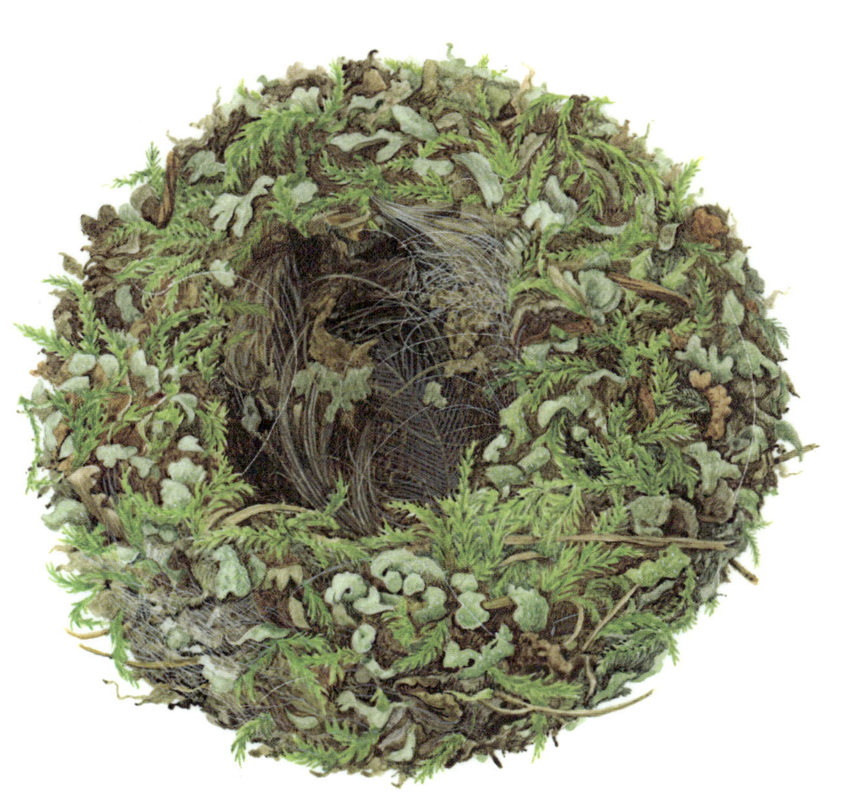

CHAFFINCH

Fringilla coelebs

One day a friend arrived at our door bearing this branch of Irish yew; I was delighted by his find, an example of just how beautifully camouflaged a chaffinch nest can be. Even with a patch of moss missing from one side it blends almost seamlessly into its surroundings.

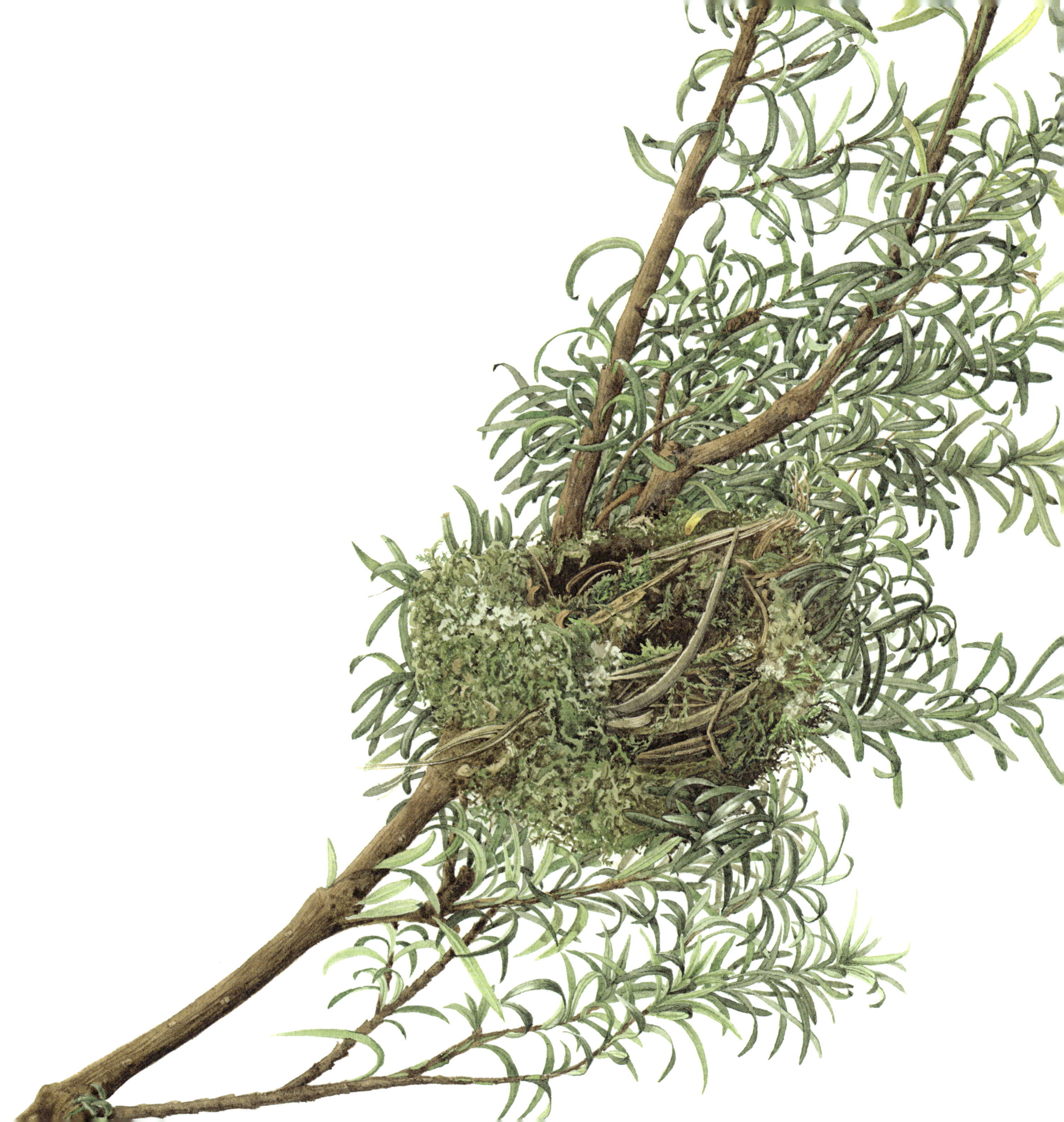

BULLFINCH

Pyrrhula pyrrhula

Resident

Lifespan — About 5 years, although 17 years has been recorded

Diet — Plant buds, invertebrates

Breeding season — April to July

Broods — 1–2 clutches of 3–6 eggs

Position — In bushes and hedges, and low tree branches

Materials — Rootlets, twigs

Lining — Horsehair, root fibres

It is always a treat to see a bullfinch, the male with his gloriously rosy breast, particularly as it is a secretive bird that rarely leaves the cover of the undergrowth.

The female builds the nest about one or two metres above ground in woodland, thickets and dense hedges. A remarkably flimsy looking structure for such a chunky little bird, it's a shallow, lacy cup of rootlets and horsehair. The hen incubates the eggs for twelve to fourteen days. Both parents feed the nestlings for twelve to eighteen days, then for a further two or three weeks near the nest site after they have fledged. The adults develop pouches on the floor of their mouths that enable them to carry larger quantities of plant buds and invertebrates to their hungry young. They often have two broods.

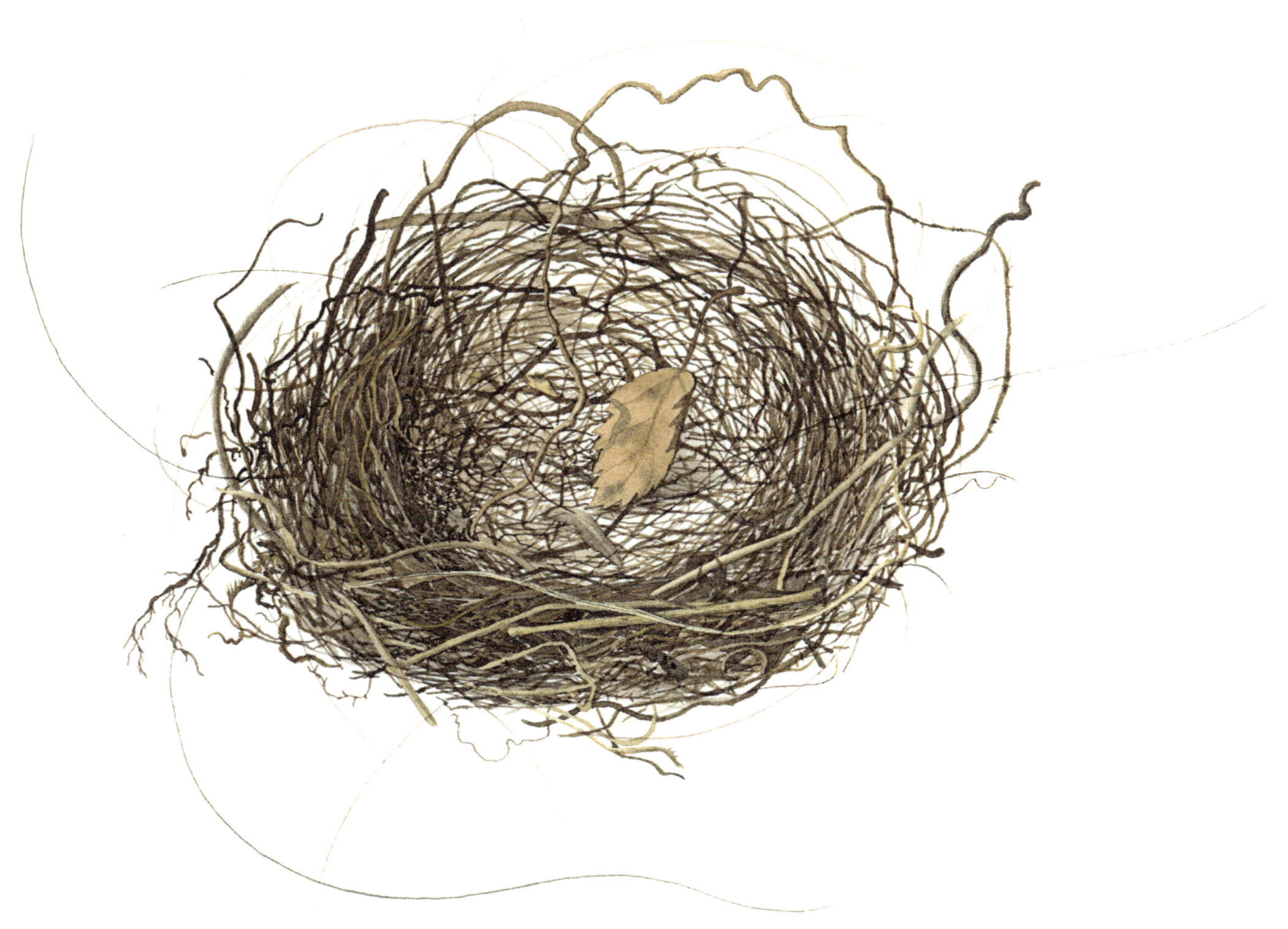

YELLOWHAMMER
Emberiza citrinella

Resident	
Lifespan	About 3 years
Diet	Seeds and grain; insects and grubs in summer
Breeding season	April to August
Broods	2–3 clutches of 3–5 eggs
Position	Near or on the ground in hedges and banks
Materials	Grasses, stems, sometimes moss
Lining	Finer grasses

The yellowhammer's habitat is extensive, from northern Scandinavia to the Mediterranean, from the British Isles to Russia. More likely to be seen in arable fields than in gardens, in winter it joins flocks of seed-eating birds visiting large fields of stubble to feed on grain left over from the harvest. In Britain its distinctive song is often rendered as 'a little bit of bread and no cheese'.

The yellowhammer's nest is made of grass, plant stems and sometimes moss, and is usually found close to the ground in hedges and banks. The female generally incubates the eggs on her own for between eleven and fourteen days, but the male helps in the feeding of the nestlings for about a fortnight until they fledge, and then for another twelve to fourteen days within the vicinity of the nest until they are independent.

One October, when the local farmers started to cut the hedges, Deon Warner went back to the place where he had watched yellowhammers during the summer and found this lovely nest.

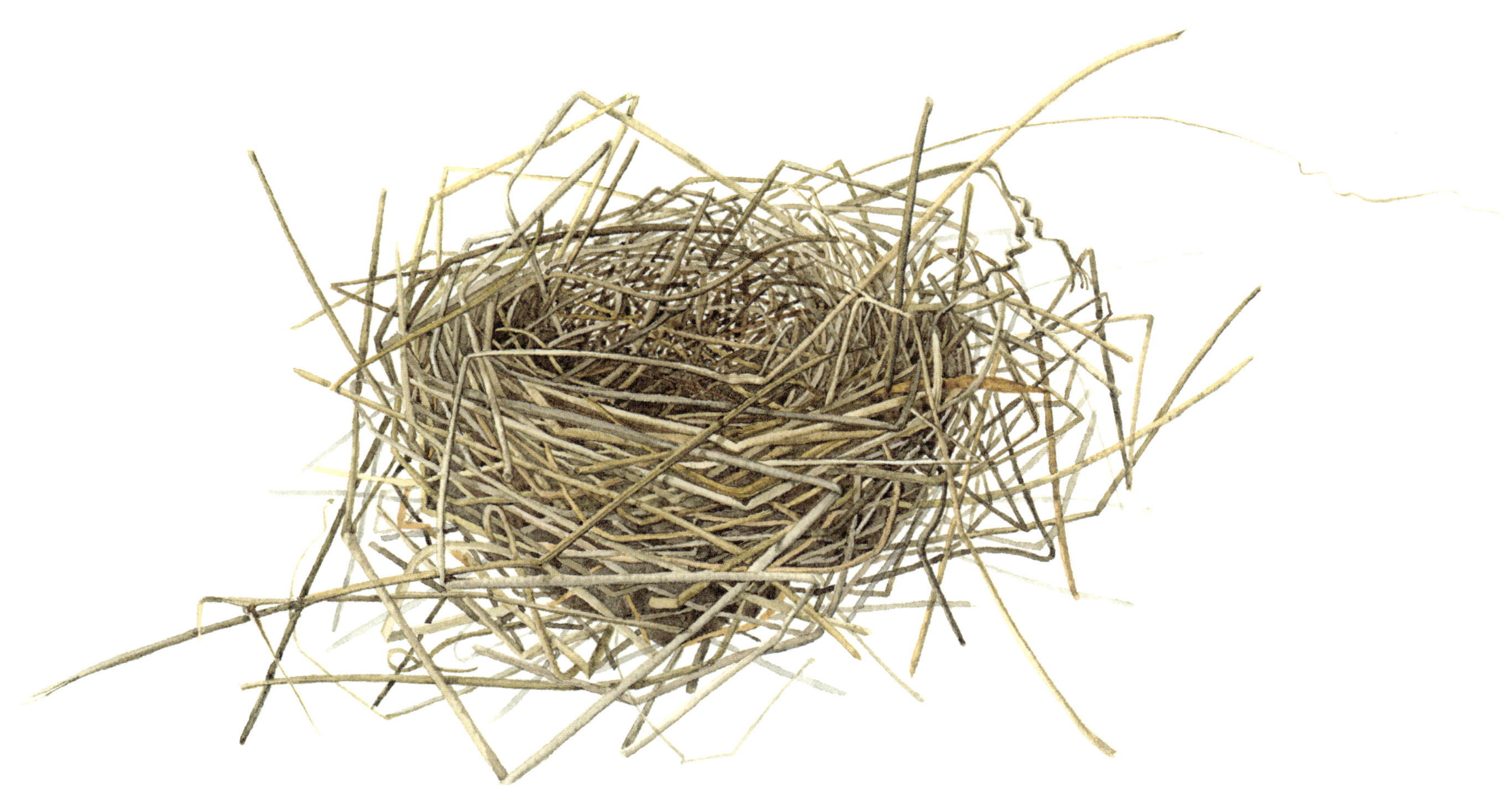

REED BUNTING
Emberiza schoeniclus

Resident

Lifespan	About 5 years, although 10 years
has been recorded

Diet	Mainly grass and wild flower seeds;
some insects

Breeding season	Late April to July

Broods	1–3 clutches of 4–7 eggs

Position	Usually near water, low down
in a bush or on the ground

Materials	Grasses, moss

Lining	Soft plant down, reed flowers,
fine grass, hair

Although the reed bunting prefers to nest near water, it also colonizes drier habitats and ditches. The female builds the nest of grasses and moss, lining it with softer materials. (This example is lined with the fluff of pulled-apart reed mace – a resourceful use of local materials.) She incubates her eggs for twelve to fourteen days, then both parents share the feeding of the young for ten to thirteen days before they fledge. They may produce three clutches in a season.

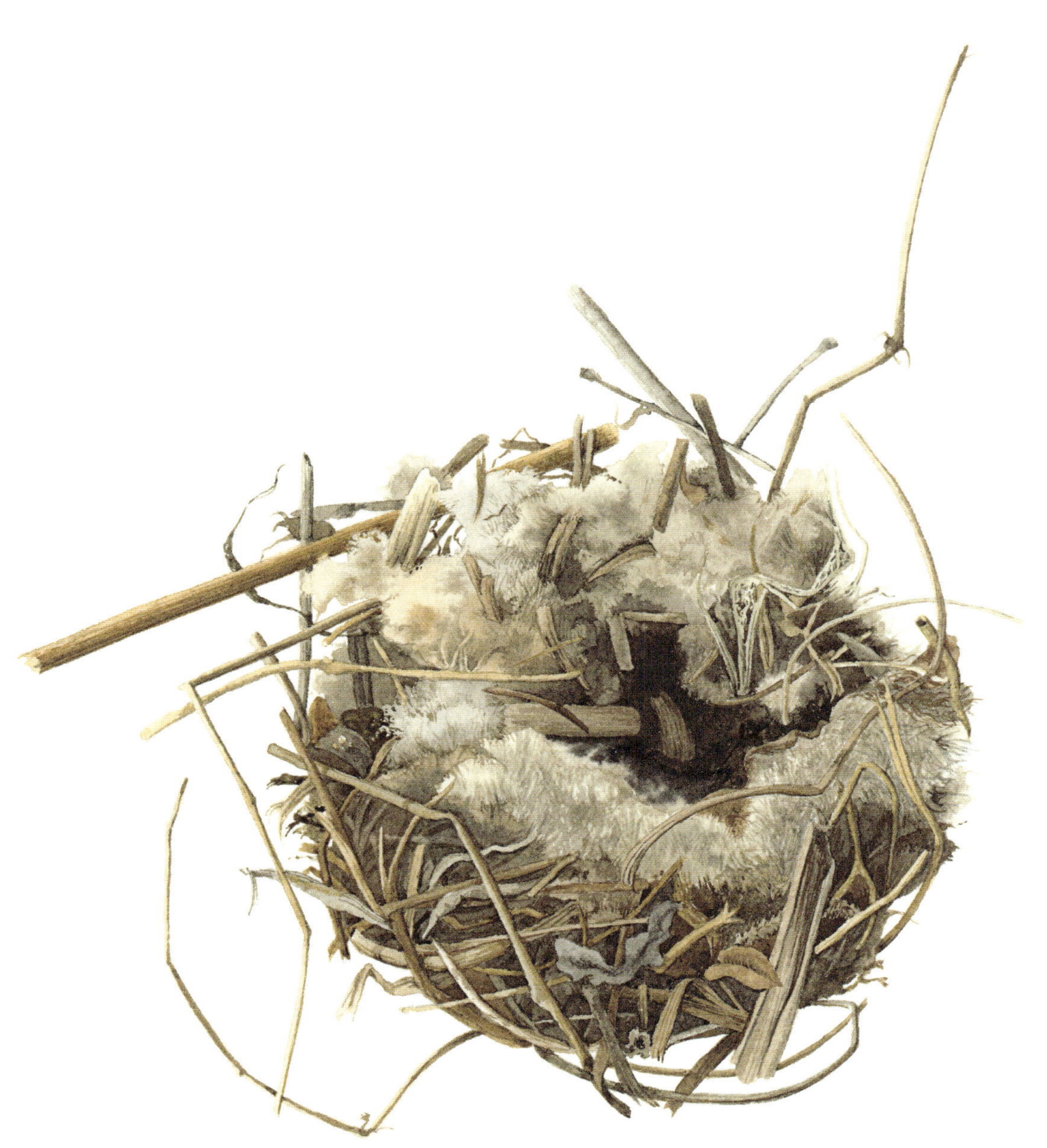

BIBLIOGRAPHY

Cerny, Walter, *A Field Guide in Colour of Birds* (London, 1975)
Ehrlich, Paul R., Dobkin, David S. and Wheye, Darryl,
    *The Birder's Handbook: A Field Guide to the Natural
    History of North American Birds* (New York, 1988)
Hall, Charles A., *Birds' Eggs and Nests* (London, 1932)
Holden, Peter and Cleeves, Tim, *RSPB Handbook of British
    Birds* (London, 2002)
Kearton, Richard, *British Birds' Nests: How, Where, and
    When to Find and Identify Them* (London, 1895)
Westell, William Percival, *Bird Life of the Seasons* (London, 1911)

ACKNOWLEDGEMENTS

It took several years to gather together and paint this collection, and none of it would have happened without my family and friends, who brought me both nests and encouragement. They are listed below; I could not have completed this work without them. I thank them all and hope they know how very grateful I am.

It will have become apparent to anyone reading this book just how huge a part has been played by Deon Warner. When I was introduced to him, early on in the project, I immediately knew I was in the right hands. Deon has found so many nests and has taught me so much about them. He has also read the script. He has been my nest guru, and I have been his very fortunate pupil. I can't thank him enough.

Thank you, too, to Jim Cassells on the Isle of Arran, who put the word about among his birdwatching friends and asked them to keep a look-out for nests.

Once the bulk of the collection was painted, two more people leapt into action and propelled me towards getting it published. My youngest son, Henry Ogilvy, urged me on, helped with research and read the text, and then he called in the help of another friend, Antonia Quirke. Antonia was a whirlwind of enthusiasm, pep talks and action, and I'm sure that I wouldn't have got anywhere without her. She and Henry put their heads together and made it all happen. Thank you both so much.

Once into the next stage I found myself in the hands of two more brilliant people – Zoë Waldie, who greeted my manuscript with such enthusiasm and then sent it on to all the right people, and Richard Atkinson, who received it so warmly from Zoë and took it from there. In his mind's eye Richard saw *Nests* just as I saw it and, true to his word, he has helped me to achieve what I set out to do. They have both been so kind and encouraging and have held my hand through every stage.

It takes many people to make a book, some of whom I have met – but far more I have not. I thank them all for their help, particularly Richard Green, Steven Lovatt, Ruth Pietroni, Sam Fulton, Imogen Scott, Corina Romonti and Liz Parsons, who have been instrumental in the designing, editing, production and marketing of this book.

And through it all my husband, Tony, has climbed ladders, packed painting equipment, driven miles and cheerfully put up with a houseful of twigs and a wife who has been mildly obsessed with nests.

I am for ever grateful to you all.

THE FINDERS

Deon Warner, Tony Ogilvy, Adam and Jo Ogilvy, Henry Ogilvy, Tom Ogilvy, Donald Easten, Philippa Harris, Fenella Harris, Utta Brown, Belinda Burne, Rosemary Brooks, Judy Burchett, Sally Nash, Neil Catchpole, Rob and Becky Cotterill, Ruth Cromie, Chris Ireland Jones, Ann Baker, Rowan Cope, Brad van Aswegen, Cicely Gill, Betty Head, Shaun Caddy, Mike Board, Su Toomer, Bob and Camilla Perry, Vickie Yates.

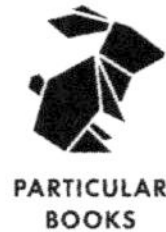

PARTICULAR
BOOKS

UK | USA | Canada | Ireland | Australia
India | New Zealand | South Africa

Particular Books is part of the Penguin Random House group of companies
whose addresses can be found at global.penguinrandomhouse.com

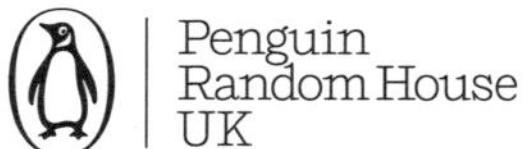

Penguin
Random House
UK

First published in Particular Books 2021
003

Copyright © Susan Ogilvy, 2021

The moral right of the author has been asserted

Designed by Richard Green

Printed in Latvia by Livonia Print

The authorized representative in the EEA is Penguin Random House Ireland,
Morrison Chambers, 32 Nassau Street, Dublin D02 YH68

A CIP catalogue record for this book is available from the British Library

ISBN: 978–0–241–48171–4

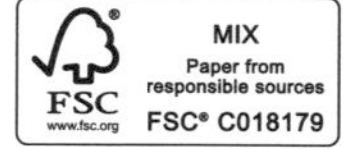

Penguin Random House is committed to a
sustainable future for our business, our readers
and our planet. This book is made from Forest
Stewardship Council® certified paper.

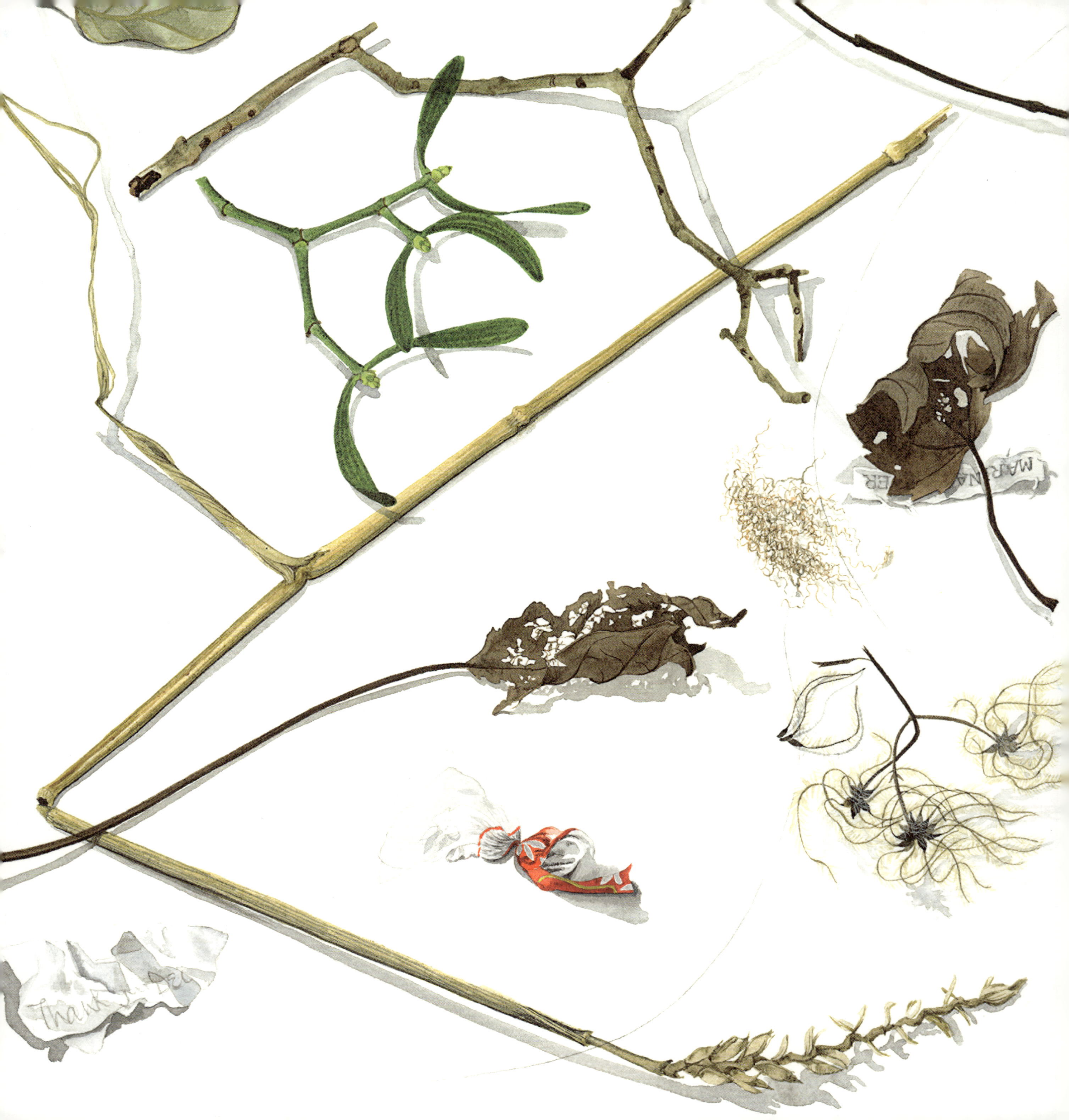
ER MARINA
thank